THE FIRST CRORE

A Roadmap for Service Business Owners

CA Ishwar Ram Yadav

notionpress.com

INDIA • SINGAPORE • MALAYSIA

ISBN
Paperback 979-8-90479-998-4
Hardcase 979-8-90479-999-1

First Edition: 2025 | Printed in India

Disclaimer: This book provides practical business guidance based on the author's professional experience. It is not a substitute for legal or financial advice. All stories are real; names and identifying details have been changed.

For every service professional who works too hard for too little—and who is finally ready to change that.

In Loving Memory of my Late Father Ram Yadav

CONTENTS

"The first crore is not the destination. It is the door."

ABOUT THE AUTHOR

CA Ishwar Ram Yadav is a practising Chartered Accountant, business growth advisor, and author based in Pune, India. With over a decade of experience working exclusively with service business owners, he has helped hundreds of entrepreneurs break through their revenue ceilings, build profitable systems, and achieve the financial freedom they set out to create.

He is the author of Penalty to Profit: GST Secrets for Manufacturing Industries, and is a sought-after speaker, coach, and advisor for service entrepreneurs across Maharashtra and beyond.

His work is built on one conviction: that every hardworking service business owner in India deserves to earn what their effort and risk are worth—and that the right guidance, applied consistently, makes that possible faster than most people believe.

He creates educational content daily on Instagram, YouTube, and LinkedIn—where thousands of business owners follow his practical, honest approach to building profitable businesses.

Connect with CA Ishwar Ram Yadav:

@caishwaryadav | linkedin.com/in/caishwaryadav | CA Ishwar Yadav on YouTube

www.kymassociates.com.com | ishwar@kymassociates.com

Also by CA Ishwar Ram Yadav:

Penalty to Profit: GST Secrets for Manufacturing Industries

Introduction

THE QUESTION NOBODY WANTS TO ANSWER

How a simple conversation changed the way I see business—and why I wrote this book

The Day I Asked the Wrong Question

It was an ordinary evening. I was sitting with one of my close friends—someone I had known for years. He ran a service business, had about fifteen to eighteen people working for him, and by all outward appearances was doing just fine. Nice office. Busy schedule. Always on the phone.

We were having tea, and I asked him something I ask almost every client, every friend, every business owner I meet.

"How much are you earning?"

He went blank.

So I tried a different angle.

"Okay, what was your turnover last year?"

Still blank.

"Alright—what is the output per team member? What does each person in your team actually bring in?"

He looked at me like I had asked him to recite the periodic table.

Here was a man running a business for years, managing nearly twenty people, staying up late, working weekends—and he had absolutely no idea what his own business was producing. Not the revenue. Not the profit. Not the efficiency of his team. Nothing.

He was not running a business. He was surviving inside one.

With fifteen to eighteen people on his payroll, his annual turnover was somewhere between one and one and a half crore rupees. That is barely enough to pay salaries, rent, and basic overheads—let alone give him the financial freedom he had been chasing all these years.

The saddest part? He thought he was doing well. Because around him, everyone else was doing the same thing. His benchmark was his neighbourhood, his peer group, his comfort zone—not his actual potential.

What We Did Next–And What Happened

I did not give him a lecture that evening. Instead, I asked him to do one simple thing: start tracking.

Make a list. Build an Excel sheet. Write down who is doing what, how much time it takes, what revenue that work generates, and what it costs. Track every rupee coming in and every rupee going out.

He resisted at first. "I am too busy," he said. Most people say that. Being busy has become a badge of honour in our culture—even when the busyness is producing nothing of real value.

But he did it. Slowly, reluctantly, he started tracking.

And what he found shocked him.

Some team members were handling work that could be automated.

Some clients were consuming eighty percent of his time but generating only twenty percent of his revenue.

Some services he was offering were actually loss-making when you counted the real cost of delivering them.

And some work—the work nobody was chasing—was quietly the most profitable thing he did.

Once we started tracking, we started making decisions. We dropped unprofitable clients. We stopped doing work that ate into margins. We restructured the team. He went from eighteen people to eight or nine—and his business not only survived, it grew. Same clients. Better service. Higher profit. Less chaos.

That is the power of working on your business instead of just working in it.

A smaller, focused team doing the right work will always outperform a large, scattered team doing everything.

This Is Not One Person's Story

Over the years, I have worked with hundreds of business owners—service industry professionals, manufacturers, traders. Chartered accountants, consultants, architects, engineers, IT firms, logistics companies, event managers, marketing agencies, coaching institutes, and more.

And across all of them, I keep seeing the same patterns.

Pattern 1: Veteran professionals earning thirty to fifty lakh rupees a year and thinking that is the ceiling. If they had taken a good corporate job instead of entrepreneurship, they would have earned the same—or more—with far less stress and zero risk.

Pattern 2: Business owners who are extremely good at their craft—great technical skills, good client relationships, solid reputation—but completely lost when it comes to pricing, hiring, systematising, and scaling.

Pattern 3: People who are chasing five clients at five lakh rupees each, when the smarter move is to serve one client at five lakhs and help that client grow to twenty-five lakhs—which benefits both of you.

Pattern 4: Owners who work like employees inside their own companies. Whatever work comes, they do. Whatever client calls, they run. There is no strategy, no plan, no goal—just reaction.

The result? Years of hard work, but no compounding. Years of effort, but no freedom. A business that depends entirely on the owner—and the moment the owner steps away, everything stops.

This is not a small problem. This is an epidemic among small and medium businesses in India.

Why I Am Writing This Book

I am a practicing professional. My core work involves compliance—GST, taxation, audits, regulatory requirements. I have authored books on GST and taxation before. That world is important. Compliance is non-negotiable. But compliance alone will not make you rich. It will keep you legal, but not necessarily free.

What I have noticed is that most business owners—especially in the service industry—get so consumed by day-to-day operations and compliance tasks that they never stop to ask the most important question:

"Am I actually building something—or just staying busy?"

This book is my attempt to answer that question. Not in a theoretical, academic way. But in a very practical, ground-level, street-smart way—based on real conversations, real businesses, and real turnarounds I have been part of.

The goal of this book is straightforward:

For service industry owners: To reach one crore rupees in annual profit—as fast as possible, as sustainably as possible.

For manufacturing and trading businesses: To reach one hundred crore rupees in annual turnover—with a clear roadmap, not luck.

These are not random numbers. They are milestones. They represent the threshold where a business stops being a survival exercise and starts becoming a genuine asset. Where the owner stops being the bottleneck and starts being the architect.

Who Should Read This Book

This book is written for you if:

> *You run a service business—a consultancy, agency, practice, firm, or professional setup—and you feel stuck at the same revenue level year after year.*
>
> *You are a manufacturer or trader who wants to break through the next turnover barrier but does not know what is holding you back.*
>
> *You are good at what you do technically, but the business side—hiring, pricing, marketing, systems—feels like a foreign language.*
>
> *You have been working hard for years but are not sure if you are actually building wealth or just generating activity.*
>
> *You want a roadmap—not inspiration, not motivation posters—but a real, practical, step-by-step guide to growth.*

This book is not for people looking for shortcuts. There are no shortcuts. But there is a smarter path. And that is what this book maps out.

How This Book Is Structured

I have built this book around the problems I hear most often from business owners. Each chapter deals with one of those problems—not as a lecture, but as a conversation. I will share real stories (with names and details changed where needed), ask you the questions you need to sit with, and give you specific actions to take.

Here is the journey we will go on together:

Chapter 1—Setting Your Goal: Why most businesses fail before they even start, and how to set a goal that actually drives behaviour.

Chapter 2—Identifying Your Niche: Why trying to serve everyone is the fastest way to grow slowly, and how to find the lane where you win.

Chapter 3—Working on Leads: Why leads die in inboxes and follow-up folders, and how to build a pipeline that converts.

Chapter 4—Pricing for Profit: Why being busy and being profitable are two completely different things, and how to fix your pricing.

Chapter 5—Hiring Your First Team: When to hire, who to hire first, and how to do it without burning your capital.

Chapter 6—Building Systems and Delegating: How to stop being the bottleneck in your own business and build a team that functions without you.

Chapter 7—The Growth Engine: How to build reputation, referrals, and revenue that compounds over time.

Chapter 8—Profit Over Turnover: How to read your numbers, protect your margins, and withdraw profit with confidence.

Chapter 9—Compliance as a Foundation: Why getting your legal and financial house in order is not a burden—it is a competitive advantage.

Chapter 10—The Power of Partnerships: How the right alliances can compress five years of growth into one.

Chapter 11—The Milestone and Beyond: What changes when you hit your first crore in profit—and how to plan the next milestone from there.

One Last Thing Before We Begin

I want to be honest with you. This book is not going to tell you that growth is easy. It is not. It will require you to change some habits, confront some uncomfortable truths about how you have been running your business, and make some decisions that may feel risky.

But I promise you this: every single idea in this book has been tested. Not in a classroom or a case study—but in real businesses, run by real people, facing real problems.

My friend with the eighteen-person team? He is now running a tighter, more profitable business with half the team and double the peace of mind. He knows his numbers now. He tracks his output. He has a goal for the year. And for the first time in years, he is excited about where his business is going.

That is what I want for you.

So let us stop drifting. Let us set a destination. And let us build the road to get there—together.

– Your Author

Practicing Professional | Business Growth Advisor

YOUR FIRST ACTION STEP

Before you read Chapter 1, answer these three questions honestly—on paper, not in your head:

1. What was my exact turnover last financial year?
2. What was my actual profit (not revenue)—after all expenses?
3. Where do I want to be financially three years from today?

If you cannot answer the first two questions today, that is okay. By the time you finish this book, you will not only know these numbers—you will know exactly what to do with them.

Chapter One

SETTING YOUR GOAL

The one habit that separated those who grew from those who just survived

Let Me Ask You Something Uncomfortable

You woke up early today. You handled calls before breakfast. You stayed late last night finishing a proposal. You have not taken a proper Sunday off in months. You have cancelled family plans, skipped vacations, and worked through festivals—all in the name of building your business.

So let me ask you this:

If you had taken a decent corporate job instead, would you be earning the same money—with half the stress?

For many business owners I meet, the honest answer is: yes.

They are earning twenty to fifty lakh rupees a year. Working twelve to fourteen hours a day. Managing staff, clients, vendors, compliance, cash flows—the whole circus. And at the end of it all, their profit is something a mid-level corporate professional could match with a predictable salary, two-day weekends, and paid leave.

That is not entrepreneurship. That is a very expensive, very stressful job—one that you gave yourself.

And the reason this happens is not lack of effort. It is not lack of talent. It is not even lack of opportunity.

It is the absence of one simple thing: a goal.

Everyone Talks About Goals. Nobody Actually Sets Them.

Ask any business owner if they believe in goal-setting and they will say yes immediately. Of course. Goals are important. Everyone knows that.

Then ask them: what is your exact profit target for this financial year?

Silence.

Not a pause. Not a moment of thought. Silence—followed by a vague answer like "I want to grow" or "We are targeting good numbers this year" or the most common one of all: "Whatever comes, we will handle."

That last one is my favourite. Whatever comes, we will handle. It sounds humble and hardworking. But what it actually means is: I have no plan. I am reacting to life instead of designing it.

A business without a goal is just a very busy person trying to catch water with their bare hands.

Here is the truth that nobody in the coaching and consulting world talks about clearly enough: setting a goal is not a motivational exercise. It is not about writing numbers on a vision board or repeating affirmations in the mirror. A real business goal is a financial commitment—to yourself, to your team, and to your future.

And when you do not make that commitment, every single decision you take is random. You take on clients you should not. You avoid hiring because you are not sure if you can afford it. You underprice your services because you have no number to work backwards from. You stay stuck—not because the market is bad, but because you have given your business no direction to move in.

The Exercise That Changed Everything For Me

Let me tell you about something I started doing a few years ago. Something so simple that when I describe it, people sometimes laugh. And then they try it—and they stop laughing.

Every year, on the first of April—the beginning of a new financial year—I sit down with two documents.

The first is my last year's Profit and Loss account. Every line. Every expense. Every source of revenue. Every number, staring back at me.

The second is a blank sheet—my projected Profit and Loss account for the year ahead.

And I do one thing: I set my goal for the year by building the P&L I want to have on 31st March next year.

Not a vague target like 'grow by 20%'.

Not a wish like 'I hope things pick up this year'.

A specific, line-by-line financial picture of what I want my business to look like twelve months from today.

Since I started doing this exercise, my profit has grown three to five times every single year. Not because I suddenly became smarter. Not because the market got easier. But because I finally had a destination—and every decision I made through the year was filtered through one question: does this take me closer to that number, or further away?

That question alone will change how you run your business.

Why This Exercise Works–The Two Things Happening at Once

When you sit down to review last year's P&L and project this year's, two very powerful things happen simultaneously—and most people miss both of them.

1. **You are forced to face the truth.** Most business owners have a rough idea of their revenue—they know how busy they were. But very few know their actual profit. The P&L exercise forces you to look at what came in, what went out, and what actually remained. That clarity, however uncomfortable, is the starting point of every good decision.
2. **Patterns reveal themselves.** When you look at last year's P&L honestly, things become visible that were invisible when you were just running from one task to the next. You can see which clients generated the most revenue.

> Which services had the best margins. Which expenses ballooned without producing results. Which months were strong and which were weak—and why. You can identify where your best leads came from, which niche gave you the highest returns, and which work you should stop doing immediately because it is costing you more than it earns.

This is not accounting. This is strategy. And the best part? You do not need to be a finance expert to do it. You just need to be honest.

The Solar Business Story: From Numbers to Strategy in One Sitting

Let me share a real example—one of my favourite ones, because it shows how beautifully simple this process can be.

I was working with a client who ran a solar energy installation business. Decent operation, good technical team, a reasonable number of clients—but he was stuck. His revenue had not grown meaningfully in two years and he had no idea why.

I asked him to bring his last year's P&L. We sat together and went through it.

Within an hour, one thing became very clear: the majority of his revenue—nearly seventy percent of it—was coming from residential household installations. Homeowners who wanted to set up solar panels. And within that group, there was a smaller set of ten to twelve clients who had not only installed themselves, but had also referred others to him over the past two years.

His best customers were not just buying from him. They were quietly selling for him—for free.

So I asked him a simple question: when did you last visit those ten clients personally?

He could not remember.

Here was my strategy for him. Not a complicated marketing plan. Not a new product launch. Just this:

> *Visit your top ten referral clients personally. Not to sell. Just to thank them.*
>
> *Show them the benefit they have received from their own solar installation—savings on electricity bills, ROI they have already seen.*
>
> *Then ask them: Do you know anyone else—a neighbour, a friend, a family member—who could benefit from the same?*
>
> *And make it easy to say yes: offer a simple gift hamper as a thank-you for every successful referral they generate.*

That is it. That was the entire strategy.

But this strategy was only visible because we had looked at the P&L first. Without the P&L, he would have spent money on digital marketing, hired a salesperson, tried new geographies—all while ignoring the goldmine that was already in his existing client base.

We set him a target: two times his previous year's profit. And we linked that target to this specific action. The goal was not just a number—it was a number with a plan attached.

He hit it.

The Minimum Standard: Why One Crore Profit Is Not Ambition–It Is Obligation

Here is something I want you to sit with.

You chose business over a job. That was not a small decision. You gave up job security, a fixed salary, leaves, weekends, and the comfort of someone else taking the big decisions. You carry risk every single day—risk of losing clients, cash flow pressure, team problems, market shifts. You carry that risk so that the reward can be proportionally larger.

So what is the minimum reward you should be earning for carrying all of that?

In my view, one crore rupees in annual profit is not an ambitious target for a service business owner. It is the minimum acceptable standard. It is the number that justifies the choice of entrepreneurship over employment. Anything below that, and you need to ask yourself a very hard question:

Am I an entrepreneur building an asset—or am I an employee who just happens to sign his own paycheques?

I say this not to be harsh, but because I have seen too many talented, hard-working people spend the best years of their life building businesses that never quite paid them what they deserved—simply because they never decided what they deserved.

The people I have seen remain stuck at twenty to thirty lakh rupees in profit for years—they are not lazy. They are not incompetent. They are working hard every single day. The problem is that they are working hard without a destination. And when you work without a destination, you work in circles.

Hard Work is Not Enough. It Never Was.

There is a very dangerous belief that circulates in the small business community—and I want to challenge it directly.

The belief is this: if I work hard enough, the results will come.

It sounds noble. It feels right. Our parents told us this. Our culture reinforces it. And in certain contexts—getting a degree, mastering a skill, building physical fitness—it is largely true.

But in business? Hard work alone is a trap.

I have met some of the hardest-working people in the world—and they are running small, struggling businesses. They are the first ones in and the last ones out. They never take a day off. And yet, year after year, the numbers stay the same.

Meanwhile, I have met business owners who seem to work fewer hours, take proper holidays, and somehow grow faster. What is the difference?

> *The hard worker is busy executing. Every day, from morning to night, doing tasks.*
>
> *The smart worker is busy deciding. Every week, reviewing numbers, making strategic choices, and delegating execution to others.*
>
> *The hard worker works IN the business. The smart worker works ON the business.*

The hard worker measures effort. The smart worker measures outcomes.

Working smart does not mean working less. It means working on the right things—and the only way to know what the right things are is to have a goal that tells you what you are working towards.

Without a goal, every task feels equally important. With a goal, suddenly some things become critical and others become distractions you can drop or delegate.

How to Set Your Goal–The Right Way

Let me give you a practical framework. Not theory. Just what I do, and what I have seen work for hundreds of business owners.

Step 1—Get last year's P&L in front of you. If you do not have one, create a simple one right now. Revenue by client or service. Expenses by category. Net profit at the bottom. This is your baseline.

Step 2—Identify the top three revenue sources. Which clients, services, or channels generated the most revenue? Which had the best margins? These are your growth engines.

Step 3—Identify the top three profit leaks. Where did money go that did not produce results? Which expenses can be reduced or eliminated? Which clients consumed the most time for the least return?

Step 4—Set your profit target for this year. Not a revenue target. A profit target. Start with the number you want to take home—let us say one crore—and then work backwards. What revenue do you need at your current margin to produce that profit? What do you need to change to hit that margin?

Step 5—Identify two or three specific actions. Like the solar business example, your P&L will reveal specific, simple strategies. Pick two or three and commit to executing them relentlessly. You do not need ten strategies. You need two that you actually follow through on.

Step 6—Review quarterly. Set a date every three months to sit with your actual P&L versus projected. Are you on track? Where are you ahead? Where are you behind? What needs to change?

That is the entire system. Six steps. One afternoon on April 1st. And a quarterly review that takes two hours. That is all it takes to go from drifting to driving.

What It Costs You to Not Have a Goal

People think that not having a goal is neutral—that it simply means you are not committed either way. But that is wrong. Not having a goal is an active choice with real consequences.

> *You take on bad clients—because you have no criteria to filter them out.*
>
> *You underprice your services—because you do not know what number you need to hit.*
>
> *You avoid investing in your team—because you are not sure if you can afford it, since you have not projected your revenue.*
>
> *You work on low-value tasks all day—because without a goal, you cannot tell the difference between high-value and low-value work.*

You stay stuck at the same revenue level year after year—not because the market is bad, but because you never decided to go higher.

Every year without a goal is a year of potential compounding that you have thrown away. And unlike money, time cannot be recovered.

The cost of not having a goal is not zero. It is everything you could have built—but did not.

Your Job is to Be a Business Owner, Not a Business Operator

I want to end this chapter with one shift in thinking that I believe is more valuable than any tactic or framework.

There are two roles inside every business. The operator and the owner. The operator does the work. The owner decides what work gets done, who does it, and where the business is going.

Most small business owners are one hundred percent operator and zero percent owner. They are so deep in the day-to-day that they never come up for air to think about the bigger picture.

Goal-setting is the act of being an owner. It is the moment when you step out of the noise, look at the horizon, and say: that is where I am going. And then you build everything in your business—your team, your pricing, your client choices, your time—around reaching that point.

You did not start a business to work yourself to exhaustion for mediocre returns. You started it for freedom, growth, and the ability to build something that outlasts you.

That starts with a number. A real, specific, written-down number.

For service businesses: one crore in annual profit.

Write it down. Put a date next to it. And let every single chapter in this book help you build the roadmap to get there.

YOUR ACTION STEP–CHAPTER 1

This week, set aside two hours. Pull out last year's Profit and Loss account—or build a simple one if you do not have it. Then answer:

1. What was my actual profit last year—not revenue, but profit after all expenses?
2. Which three clients or services generated the most value?
3. Which three expenses or activities produced the least value?
4. What is my profit target for this financial year? Write the exact number.
5. What are two specific actions—like the solar referral strategy—that my P&L suggests I should take right now?

Do not move to Chapter 2 until you have a number. A real number. Because everything that follows is built on it.

*

Coming up in Chapter 2:

Identifying Your Niche—Why trying to serve everyone is the fastest way to grow slowly

Chapter Two

IDENTIFYING YOUR NICHE

Why trying to serve everyone is the fastest way to grow slowly—and how to find the lane where you win

When I Was Doing Everything–And Excelling at Nothing

There was a time, not so long ago, when I was the definition of a busy professional.

I was a practising Chartered Accountant, and I was doing everything I possibly could. Filing GST returns. Filing income tax returns. Filing TDS returns. Handling project work. Taking on audit assignments. Advising clients on compliance. Whenever a client asked me if I could help with something, my answer was almost always yes—because every yes meant more revenue, and more revenue meant growth. Or so I thought.

I was serving clients from every industry. Manufacturing. Trading. Real estate. Retail. Services. Healthcare. Whatever came my way, I took it. I was targeting every friend, every contact, every referral—anyone who could put money in my pocket.

From the outside, it looked like a thriving practice.

From the inside, it was chaos.

I was busy every single day. But I had no idea what I was actually building.

The problems started showing up in ways I could not ignore.

First, my team. Because we were working across so many different industries and so many different types of work, my team could not be trained for any one thing deeply. There was no specialisation, no standard process, no expertise that could be repeated efficiently. Every new client was a new learning curve—for me and for them.

Which meant that whenever a complex client issue came up, I could not simply delegate it. I had to sit with it personally. I had to research. I had to read new regulations, understand new industry dynamics, figure out new solutions—every single time, for every single client.

A task that should have taken one hour was taking two days. A problem that a specialised team could have solved in an afternoon was consuming my entire week.

I was not running a business. I was running a hundred small businesses simultaneously—and doing justice to none of them.

The Lesson That Changed Everything

A few years into this chaos, I made one of the best decisions of my professional life: I invested in a business coaching programme.

I went in expecting to learn about marketing, sales, and scaling. What I got instead was something far more foundational.

The first—and most important—lesson my coach gave me was this:

Stop trying to be everything to everyone. Decide who you serve, what you solve, and how you deliver it. Then do only that.

It sounds so simple when you read it. But for someone who had built an identity around saying yes to everything, it felt almost frightening.

If I narrow down, will I not lose clients? Will I not miss opportunities? Will my revenue not shrink before it grows?

My coach smiled and said: "Your revenue might slow for three months. But your growth will accelerate for the next thirty years."

He was right.

What Niching Down Actually Did For My Practice

After that coaching journey, I made a clear decision. My practice would focus on service and manufacturing businesses. Within that, we would offer three specific things: helping them grow their business strategically, solving their GST and compliance challenges, and helping them access the right loans and financial products.

That is it. Three services. Two industries. A clear, defined lane.

The transformation was not just visible in revenue—it was visible in everything.

My team could now be trained deeply for a specific type of work. They did not need to figure out every client from scratch. They had SOPs—Standard Operating Procedures—that we had built from experience across dozens of similar clients.

A client that previously took me two to three days to onboard and handle can now be set up in one to two hours. I review the SOPs, customise where needed, and my team executes.

My confidence went through the roof. Because I had now worked with over three hundred businesses in my niche, I knew their problems before they told me. I knew the strategies that worked and the ones that did not. I was no longer a generalist trying to figure things out—I was a specialist who had already figured them out.

And clients could feel the difference. When you walk into a meeting knowing more about a client's industry than they do, the conversation changes completely. You are not a vendor anymore. You are a trusted advisor.

That is the compounding power of niche. Every client you serve in your chosen space makes you better at serving the next one. Your knowledge deepens. Your systems sharpen. Your reputation grows. And eventually, you become the go-to person for that specific problem in that specific industry—and that is when business starts coming to you instead of you chasing it.

What a Niche Is–And What It Is Not

Before we go further, I want to clear up a very common misconception—one I hear constantly from consultants, coaches, and service providers.

"My niche is social media marketing."

"My niche is digital marketing."

"My niche is HR consulting."

No. That is not a niche. That is a service. And there is a fundamental difference.

A niche is the intersection of three things: the industry you serve, the problem you solve, and the way you deliver the solution. All three together define your niche. Just one of them is simply a category.

Not a niche: "I do social media marketing."

A niche: "I help mid-sized manufacturing companies build their LinkedIn presence to attract B2B buyers and distributors."

Not a niche: "I do HR consulting."

A niche: "I help service businesses with ten to fifty employees build their first hiring and onboarding systems so the founder can stop doing everything themselves."

Not a niche: "I do accounting and compliance."

A niche: "I help service and manufacturing businesses navigate GST challenges, grow strategically, and access the right financial products."

See the difference? The niche version tells you exactly who it is for, what problem it solves, and what outcome it delivers. The generalist version could apply to anyone—which means it attracts no one in particular.

If your business description could apply to a thousand other people, you do not have a niche. You have a job title.

Your Name Should Tell the Story

Think about the brands and names you respect most in business. When someone mentions them, you immediately know what they stand for.

Zerodha—share market investing for everyday Indians

Zomato—food delivery at your doorstep

Practo—doctors and healthcare, online

Delhivery—logistics and last-mile delivery

None of these brands try to be everything. Each one is deeply associated with one problem, one solution, one promise. And that association—that clarity in the market's mind—is worth more than any amount of advertising.

Now ask yourself honestly: when someone takes your name in a professional conversation, what do they think of? What do they say you do? Is there a clear, immediate answer? Or do people describe you as "that person who does all kinds of business work"?

If it is the latter, you do not yet have a niche. And that is costing you clients, revenue, and reputation—every single day.

The goal is for your name—or your brand name—to become synonymous with one specific type of expertise. So that when a business owner in your target industry has that specific problem, your name is the first one that comes to mind.

That level of recognition does not come from doing more things. It comes from doing one thing, exceptionally well, for a long time.

Do One Thing a Thousand Times

There is an old principle in skill development: to achieve mastery, you need deep repetition. Not variety. Not exploration. Deep, focused repetition in a specific area.

This applies to businesses just as powerfully as it applies to individuals.

When you serve the same type of client with the same type of problem repeatedly, something remarkable happens. The first time, it takes you ten hours to solve. The fifth time, seven hours. The twentieth time, three hours. The hundredth time, one hour—and your solution is better than it was at ten hours, because you have refined it through experience.

Your delivery time shrinks.

Your quality improves.

Your team becomes self-sufficient in this area.

Your pricing power increases because you are now the expert, not a generalist.

Your referrals multiply because satisfied clients refer others with the same problem.

And your confidence—in meetings, in proposals, in conversations—is unmistakable.

That is what happened in my practice. Today, when I sit with a manufacturing or service business owner, I already know the top ten problems they are likely facing before they open their mouth. I know what has worked for similar businesses. I know the regulatory traps they are walking towards. I know the growth levers that are sitting unused.

That knowledge did not come from reading. It came from repetition—from serving the same niche deeply, again and again, until the patterns became instinct.

You cannot buy that expertise. You can only earn it through focused repetition in a chosen niche.

How to Actually Identify Your Niche

Here is where most people get stuck. They understand the concept of niche intellectually—but when it comes to deciding their own, they freeze. They worry about getting it wrong. They worry about leaving money on the table. They overthink.

Let me simplify it for you. Your niche is not something you invent. It is something you discover—by looking at what you have already done.

Go back to your Profit and Loss account from Chapter 1. It is about to become useful again.

1. **Look at your client list.** Write down every client you served in the last one to two years. Next to each name, write the industry they are in and the type of work you did for them.
2. **Identify which clients gave you the highest revenue.** Not the most work—the highest revenue. These are the

clients whose fees were largest relative to the time you spent.

3. **Identify which clients took the least effort.** Which engagements felt smooth? Where did you finish the work quickly and confidently, without extensive research or stress? These clients were in your zone of competence.
4. **Identify which industry you genuinely enjoy working in.** This matters more than most people admit. When you enjoy the industry, you learn faster, you stay curious, and you bring energy to client conversations that clients can feel. Passion is not a luxury—it is a competitive advantage.
5. **Look for the overlap.** Where do high revenue, low effort, and genuine interest meet? That overlap—that sweet spot—is your niche. It is where you are already performing best, without even trying.
6. **Ask: can I add more value here than anywhere else?** The final test. In this niche, with your experience and knowledge, can you genuinely solve problems that others cannot? Can you see things that a generalist would miss? If yes—this is your lane.

Once you have identified that overlap, everything becomes clearer. Your marketing speaks directly to one type of person. Your team trains deeply in one area. Your proposals become more confident. Your pricing goes up because you are a specialist, not a commodity.

The Fear That Holds Everyone Back–And Why It Is Wrong

I know what you are thinking right now. Because I thought the same thing when my coach first pushed me towards niching down.

"If I narrow my focus, I will lose the clients who do not fit my niche. My revenue will drop. I will be turning away work."

This fear is completely understandable—and almost completely wrong.

Here is what actually happens when you niche down.

You stop wasting time on low-margin, high-effort clients who were never going to help you grow anyway.

You start attracting better clients—clients who specifically want the type of expertise you have built, and who are willing to pay a premium for it.

You stop competing on price. Generalists compete on price because they have no other differentiator. Specialists compete on expertise—and expertise commands higher fees.

You build a reputation in one space, which generates referrals from within that community. People who know the same type of people refer you naturally.

You get your time back. Because your team can handle more without you, because your systems are built for a specific type of work, and because you are no longer spending days researching industries you barely know.

Yes, in the first few months of niching down, you may turn away some work that does not fit your new focus. That requires discipline. But within six to twelve months, the revenue you lost is replaced by better revenue—from better clients, with better margins, with less effort.

I have seen this happen with enough business owners now to say it with complete confidence: niching down is not a risk. Staying a generalist is the risk.

The generalist chases every opportunity. The specialist attracts the right ones.

Your Niche Is Your Identity

Let me close this chapter with a thought I want you to carry forward.

In business, clarity is confidence. And the clearest statement you can make—to the market, to your clients, and to yourself—is this: I serve this type of person, with this type of problem, in this specific way. Better than anyone else.

That statement is your niche. And it is the foundation of every good decision you will make about your business from this point forward.

Which clients to take on. Which to politely decline. Which team members to hire. Which skills to develop. Which services to offer. Which to retire.

All of it flows from your niche.

Once I found mine, I stopped being a busy professional trying to do everything. I became a trusted expert who knew one space deeply—and that distinction changed my business, my income, and my life.

It will do the same for you.

YOUR NICHE DISCOVERY ASSIGNMENT

Set aside one hour. Pull out your client list from the last two years and your P&L from Chapter 1. Then complete this exercise:

Step 1: List every client you served. Next to each, write their industry and the type of work you did.

Step 2: Circle the three clients who gave you the highest revenue relative to the time invested.

Step 3: Put a star next to the three clients whose work felt the smoothest and most confident.

Step 4: Underline the two or three industries you genuinely enjoy working in.

Step 5: Look for overlap between your circled, starred, and underlined entries. Write down the pattern you see.

Step 6: Complete this sentence and read it aloud: "I help ________ businesses solve ________ so that they can ________."

That sentence—if it is specific, honest, and based on your real strengths—is your niche statement. It is the beginning of your brand identity. Polish it. Test it in conversations. Refine it over the next thirty days. And then build everything in your business around it.

*

Coming up in Chapter 3:

Working on Leads—Why most leads die in inboxes, and how to build a pipeline that actually converts

Chapter Three

WORKING ON LEADS

Leads will not come to you. You have to go to them—and here is exactly how

The Conversation That Stopped Me in My Tracks

I was sitting with a close friend of mine—an interior designer with genuine talent, a solid portfolio, and years of experience. He had done beautiful work for some well-known clients. His referrals were good. His execution was reliable.

But that evening, he was not talking about any of that. He was venting.

For fifteen, twenty minutes, I just listened. He talked about leads. Or rather, the lack of them. How he was working so hard. How he was delivering everything to his existing clients. How he was calling people, following up, trying his best—and still, new leads were not coming. His business had plateaued and he could not figure out why.

Leads, leads, leads. That was the entire conversation.

I let him finish. And then I asked him one question.

"How many new people have you actually met in the last thirty days?"

He paused.

"Many," he said. "I meet people all the time."

"Not your regular clients," I said. "Not people you already know. New people. People you met for the first time, for the specific purpose of growing your business. How many?"

He thought about it.

"Two," he said.

Two people. In thirty days.

And then he wondered why leads were not coming.

The Real Problem Is Not the Leads. It Is the Mindset.

Here is the honest truth that most business owners do not want to hear: leads do not have a problem finding businesses that deserve them. The problem is that most business owners are waiting for leads to arrive instead of going out to find them.

There are two fundamentally different ways of looking at business—and at life itself.

Life happens TO you	**vs**	**You make life happen**
You wait for clients to refer someone	→	**You go out and ask clients for referrals**
You hope someone remembers you	→	**You stay visible so they cannot forget you**

You expect work to come your way	→	**You create the conditions for work to come**
You react to opportunities	→	**You generate opportunities**
You measure effort	→	**You measure meetings, calls, and referrals**

My interior designer friend was a first-type person—talented, hardworking, but waiting for the world to recognise him and send clients his way. And many, many business owners are exactly like him. They put all their energy into delivering great work—which is important—but zero energy into the systematic activity of generating new business.

Great work is necessary. But it is not sufficient. It will get you referrals occasionally, when a happy client happens to remember you at exactly the right moment when someone they know needs your service. That is a lottery. And you cannot build a business on a lottery.

Your first crore will not come from waiting. It will come from walking out of your office and meeting people—deliberately, consistently, relentlessly.

The Goldmine You Are Already Sitting On

Before we talk about digital marketing, paid ads, or any expensive lead generation strategy—let me tell you where your first crore of revenue is hiding.

It is in your phone. Right now.

Every person in your contact list is a potential lead, a referral source, or a connector to someone who needs exactly what you offer. Your existing clients, your old colleagues, your college friends who are now running businesses, the vendors you work with, the people you met at networking events two years ago and never followed up with—all of them.

Most service business owners have two hundred, three hundred, sometimes four hundred or more people in their contact book who they have not spoken to in months or years. That is not a dead database. That is a dormant goldmine.

> *You do not need a digital marketing agency to reach these people.*
>
> *You do not need to spend money on Meta ads to get in front of them.*
>
> *You just need to pick up the phone, send a message, and ask for a coffee meeting.*

That is it. That is the entire strategy for your first phase of lead generation.

Go through your contact list. Identify people who are business owners, decision-makers, or well-connected individuals in your target niche. Reach out—not to sell, but to reconnect. Ask them how business is going. Listen. And then, when the moment is right, ask one simple question:

"Do you know anyone who might be facing this kind of problem? I would love to connect with them."

That one question, asked consistently across fifty or a hundred conversations, will generate more leads than six months of social media posts.

"I Don't Have Time"–The Most Expensive Excuse in Business

When I said this to my interior designer friend, his response was immediate.

"Sir, I have no time. I am running everywhere. I cannot spare an hour for meetings."

I looked at him for a moment. And then I said something that I think landed harder than he expected.

"You are doing fifty lakh rupees of business. You cannot spare one hour a day? That is not a time problem. That is an operations problem. And if your operations are so broken that the owner cannot take out one hour to grow the business, then fixing operations is the more urgent priority."

He went quiet.

If your business is so dependent on you that you cannot spare one hour a day to grow it—your business owns you. You do not own it.

One hour a day. Three meetings a week. That is the minimum standard for lead generation activity in a service business.

Not three meetings every month when you feel like it. Three meetings every single week—in your calendar, protected, non-negotiable.

Think about what three meetings a week means over a year. That is more than a hundred and fifty meaningful conversations with potential clients or referral sources. Even if only ten percent of those lead to new business, that is fifteen new client relationships. For most service businesses, fifteen good new clients in a year would represent serious, meaningful growth.

All from one hour a day. Three meetings a week. Coffee, a phone call, or a thirty-minute sit-down.

The Lead Sheet–Your Most Underrated Business Tool

Here is where most business owners lose the game even when they are doing the right things.

Someone refers a potential client. You take their name. You say you will follow up. And then two weeks go by, you get busy, and you never call. The referral goes cold. The opportunity disappears.

Or worse—a client mentions a colleague who might need your services. You nod. You intend to follow up. But you did not write it down anywhere, and by the next morning it is gone.

This is not a memory problem. This is a system problem. And the solution is embarrassingly simple.

A lead sheet.

Not a sophisticated CRM software. Not an expensive digital platform. Just a simple, maintained list—in Excel, in a notebook, anywhere—that captures every potential lead and every follow-up action required.

Column 1—Name: Who is the potential client or referral?

Column 2—Source: Who referred them or how did you find them?

Column 3—Contact details: Phone, email, whatever you have.

Column 4—What they need: What is the problem or service they might require?

Column 5—Last contact date: When did you last speak or reach out?

Column 6—Next action: What needs to happen next, and by when?

Column 7—Status: New lead / In conversation / Proposal sent / Converted / Not interested.

Every morning—before you open your email, before you start your day—spend ten minutes looking at this sheet. Ask yourself one question: is there a meeting I can schedule today? Is there a follow-up call I can make this morning?

The lead sheet does something powerful that most people underestimate. It makes your pipeline visible. Right now, your leads are scattered across your memory, your WhatsApp, your email, and your head. When something lives only in your head, it is invisible—and you cannot manage what you cannot see.

When your leads are on a sheet, they are real. They have names. They have statuses. They have actions pending. And every morning, the sheet reminds you that your business growth depends on these names—not on luck.

The Art of Asking–Why Most People Come Back Empty-Handed

Here is a pattern I see constantly. A business owner goes to a networking event, or meets a client for coffee, has a great conversation—and comes back with nothing. No leads. No referrals. No new connections.

And the reason, almost always, is this: they never asked.

They talked about their services. They gave their card. They had a lovely chat. But they never asked a specific, clear, easy-to-answer question that could lead to a referral.

Let me show you the difference between how most people ask and how it should be done.

> *WRONG: "If you know anyone who needs my services, please do refer them."*
>
> *This is vague. It puts the entire burden on the other person to think of someone, evaluate whether they need your services, and remember to tell you. It almost never works.*
>
> *RIGHT: "I work with manufacturing businesses to help them get loans at 10.5% interest—better rates than most people know are available. Do you know two or three manufacturing business owners I could have a brief conversation with? I can help them save significantly on their borrowing costs."*

See the difference? The second version is specific about who you are looking for, what problem you solve, and what value the referred person will receive. It makes it easy for the other person to think of names immediately.

But even then, the conversation does not end there. Because most people, when asked, will say: "Yes, I know a few people. Let me think about it and get back to you."

And then they forget. Life gets busy. The intention was genuine but the follow-through never happened.

So I have one more step I always use. I say:

"I completely understand. But while we are here, can you just give me two or three names? I will take it from there—you do not need to make any calls on my behalf. I will reach out myself and mention your name."

Most people can give you names on the spot if you ask them that way. And once you have names, you have leads. The rest is follow-up.

I always follow up two to three days later with a simple message: "Have you had a chance to connect those names with me? No pressure—just wanted to check in." That gentle reminder, more often than not, gets me the introductions.

People will not give you referrals without being asked. And most people will not follow through without a gentle reminder. Asking and following up are not pushy—they are professional.

Digital Presence–Not a Strategy, But a Support System

Let me be very clear about something before we go further. For your first crore of revenue, digital marketing is not your primary lead generation engine. Your network, your meetings, and your referrals are.

But digital presence plays a supporting role that is important and easy to underestimate.

Here is what it does: it keeps you visible to the people who already know you. When a past client or a contact sees your post on LinkedIn or WhatsApp, it reminds them that you exist, that you are active, and that you are an expert in your space. And when someone they know asks for a recommendation in your category—they think of you.

That is all your digital presence needs to do at this stage. Not generate cold leads. Not go viral. Just remind your existing network that you are there.

The bar for this is much lower than most people think.

> *Post something useful in your niche once or twice a week—a short insight, a client result (with permission), a question, a lesson from your work.*
>
> *Be consistent. Three posts a week for six months beats a burst of daily posts followed by two months of silence.*
>
> *Write for your ideal client—the person you identified in Chapter 2. Speak directly to their problems. Do not try to impress everyone.*
>
> *Engage genuinely when people comment or respond. A conversation in the comments is worth ten silent views.*

You do not need a social media manager for this. You do not need professional photography or a content calendar. You need ten minutes a day and something genuine to say about the work you do.

The combination of consistent offline meetings and consistent online visibility creates a powerful effect: people see you everywhere, in their feed and in person, and you become the obvious first choice when the need arises.

Why Your Niche and Your Lead Strategy Must Be Aligned

Here is something that trips up even business owners who understand lead generation intellectually: they go to networking events, meet people, have great conversations—and still come back with nothing. Because they were meeting the wrong people.

This is why Chapter 2 had to come before Chapter 3.

Your niche defines who your ideal client is. And your lead generation activity should be entirely focused on finding and building relationships with people who fit that profile—or who know people who do.

If you are an interior designer who works primarily with high-end residential projects, your lead activity should be focused on meeting real estate developers, premium furniture vendors, architects, and wealthy homeowners—not generic business networking groups full of people from every industry.

If you are like me—working with manufacturing and service businesses on growth, compliance, and loans—then every meeting I take, every referral I ask for, every piece of content I post is targeted at that specific audience. I am not trying to be visible to everyone. I am trying to be unforgettable to the right people.

Random networking is a time-wasting activity. Targeted networking, in your niche, is a growth strategy.

Before every meeting, every event, every outreach—ask yourself: is this person, or this room, full of my ideal clients or people who know my ideal clients? If the answer is no, spend that time on something that is.

Three Things That Will Transform Your Lead Pipeline

Let me bring everything in this chapter to a simple, executable summary. Three things. If you do all three consistently, your lead problem will be solved within ninety days.

1. **Go out and meet people—deliberately.** Three meetings a week, minimum. Target people in your niche or who know people in your niche. Go for coffee, a phone call, a thirty-minute sit-down. Not to sell—to connect, to listen, and to ask one good referral question before you leave.
2. **Maintain your lead sheet—religiously.** Every lead goes on the sheet. Every follow-up has a date. Every morning, spend ten minutes reviewing it. The sheet is your business pipeline. If it is empty, you are not doing enough meetings. If it is full of stale entries you never followed up on, you are losing business every single day.
3. **Stay visible online—consistently.** Post something useful in your niche two to three times a week. Not to generate viral content—just to stay top of mind with your existing network. Two months of consistent,

genuine posts will do more for your recall value than a year of sporadic activity.

These three things cost almost nothing. No ad budget. No agency. No complicated technology. Just consistency, discipline, and the willingness to go out and have conversations.

My interior designer friend, by the way, took this advice. He started tracking his meetings. He committed to three new meetings a week. He started posting his project work on Instagram and LinkedIn twice a week. And within sixty days, he had more leads in his pipeline than he had seen in the previous six months.

Not because the market changed. Because he changed how he showed up in the market.

YOUR ACTION STEP–CHAPTER 3

This week, do these three things—no excuses, no delays:

Action 1: Open your contact list right now. Identify twenty people who are business owners or well-connected professionals in your target niche. Write their names down. These are your first twenty outreach conversations.

Action 2: Build your lead sheet today. It can be a simple Excel file or even a notebook. Set it up with the seven columns described in this chapter. Move every existing lead or referral you have been carrying in your head onto this sheet immediately.

Action 3: Schedule three meetings for this week. Not next week—this week. One existing client to ask for referrals. One new person from your contact list. One networking event or industry gathering where your target clients are likely to be.

Action 4: Post something useful in your niche on WhatsApp or LinkedIn today. One insight, one question, one result from a recent project. Keep it simple. Just start.

Remember: your first crore is hiding in your contact book. You just have to go and find it.

*

Coming up in Chapter 4:

Pricing for Profit—Why being busy and being profitable are two completely different things

Chapter Four

PRICING FOR PROFIT

Why charging less is not helping your client—and what happens when you finally charge what you are worth

The Man Who Was Leaving Money–and Quality–on the Table

I was sitting with a client of mine who runs a construction business. Good contractor. Solid reputation. Clients liked his work. He had been in the business for years.

In his line of work, pricing is typically quoted per square foot. When I looked at the market, I found contractors charging two thousand, twenty-five hundred rupees per square foot and more. Premium players, certainly—but not rare. Not out of reach for a competent, experienced contractor.

My client was charging fourteen hundred rupees per square foot.

I asked him why.

His answer was simple. "Sir, if I charge more, clients will go elsewhere. They will not pay."

I have heard some version of this answer hundreds of times. From architects. From consultants. From designers, coaches, accountants, trainers, developers, and marketing professionals. The industries change. The words change slightly. But the fear underneath is always the same.

"If I charge more, they will not pay." This one belief is costing you more than any bad client or slow market ever could.

Why We Are Afraid to Charge What We Are Worth

Let me say something that might feel uncomfortable—because it is true, and it is important.

Most of us come from middle-class backgrounds where money was never something to be displayed, celebrated, or aggressively pursued. Earning enough was virtuous. Earning a lot was suspicious. Wanting more was greedy. Charging more than the person next to you was almost unseemly.

Those values shaped good people. But they make for terrible pricing strategies.

Because when you carry that conditioning into your business, you start treating every pricing conversation like a moral test rather than a business negotiation. You feel guilty charging premium fees. You pre-emptively lower your price before the client has even objected. You accept whatever number makes the discomfort go away—even if it is a number that slowly bleeds your business dry.

You fear losing the client, so you lower your price.

You fear being judged as greedy, so you stay quiet about your value.

You fear rejection, so you make yourself easy to say yes to—by making yourself cheap.

And in doing all of this, you build a business that can never grow, never hire well, and never deliver the quality that would justify better pricing in the first place.

Here is the thing I want you to understand. The day you decided to quit your job and start your business—that was a bold decision. You chose risk over security. You chose the harder path because you wanted something the easier path could not give you: financial freedom, creative fulfilment, time on your own terms, and the ability to build something of your own.

That decision deserves to be honoured. Not by working for fourteen hundred rupees a square foot when you are worth twenty-five hundred. But by standing up for the value you genuinely deliver—and charging accordingly.

You did not leave the safety of a job to build a struggling business. Charge like you believe in what you do.

The Cycle That Traps Every Underpriced Business

Here is the argument I want to make carefully, because it is one that many people hear but few truly internalise: charging less is not helping your client. It is harming them.

That sounds counterintuitive. Let me explain it with a chain of cause and effect.

- You charge low fees to win the client and avoid rejection.
- Low fees mean thin margins—not enough money to invest in your business.
- With thin margins, you cannot afford to hire good, experienced staff.
- So you hire cheap staff—who are either inexperienced, unmotivated, or both.
- Cheap staff deliver inconsistent, lower-quality work.
- You end up deeply involved in every project because you cannot trust the team.
- You are buried in operations—no time to go out and find new leads.
- Without new leads, revenue stagnates. Pressure increases.
- You take on more clients at low fees just to cover costs.
- You are busier than ever, earning less than you should, delivering work below your potential.
- The client—who wanted quality—ends up paying a cheap fee for mediocre output, and long-term, this costs them more than a higher fee for better work would have.

That is the underpricing trap. It is a circle—and once you are in it, it is very hard to get out. Because every time you try to raise your prices, your business is so stretched and your team so underprepared that you cannot actually justify the higher price with better delivery.

The only way out is to break the circle. And the break happens at the top—by deciding, right now, that you will charge what you are worth.

What Happens When You Charge Premium Fees

Now let me show you what the opposite cycle looks like.

- You charge premium fees—a price that reflects the real value you deliver.
- Healthy margins give you the ability to invest in your business.
- You hire good, experienced, motivated staff.
- Good staff deliver high-quality work consistently—without you in every detail.
- You are freed from daily operations and can focus on strategy and growth.
- You have time to go out, meet clients, build relationships, generate new leads.
- New leads come in. You can choose the best clients—not just any client.
- Better clients with higher budgets allow you to do your best, most creative work.
- Your reputation grows. Premium clients refer other premium clients.
- Your business compounds—revenue grows, quality improves, stress decreases.
- The client receives outstanding work that delivers real, lasting value. They are happy to have paid the premium.

This is not theory. This is what I have watched happen in practice after practice, business after business, when an owner finally had the courage to charge what they were worth.

Premium pricing is not just good for you. It is good for your client.

When you charge what you are worth, you can afford to deliver what your client deserves. Underpricing is a disservice—to yourself and to them.

Stop Pricing Your Time. Start Pricing Your Value.

Here is one of the most important mindset shifts in this entire book.

Most service business owners price based on time. How many hours will this take? What is my hourly rate? Multiply the two, add a small margin, and that is the quote.

This approach has one fundamental flaw: it makes your expertise worthless.

Let me give you an example from my own practice. Suppose I am handling a GST litigation case. The case involves a company that has received a tax notice demanding a payment of ten crore rupees. I have handled many cases like this. I know the law, I know the precedents, and I know exactly how to structure the defence. What would have taken a junior consultant three weeks of research, I can resolve with clarity in a few focused sessions.

Now—should I charge for the hours I spent? Or for the ten crore rupees I helped the client save?

> **TIME-BASED PRICING**
>
> I spent fifteen hours on this. My hourly rate is three thousand rupees. Total fee: forty-five thousand rupees. The client saved ten crore rupees and paid forty-five thousand for it. I undervalued myself by an extraordinary margin.
>
> **VALUE-BASED PRICING**
>
> The client's exposure was ten crore rupees. My intervention resolved it entirely. The fee I charge should reflect the magnitude of the problem solved—not the hours on my clock. A fee of five to ten lakhs for saving ten crores is entirely reasonable and fair to both sides.

This principle applies across every service business, not just professional practices.

An interior designer working with a client whose budget is ten lakh rupees cannot charge the same fees as one working with a client whose budget is one crore rupees—even if the hours are similar. Because the value created, the scale of work, the quality of team required, and the outcome for the client are completely different.

If you work with the one-crore client and charge premium fees, you can devote your best team, your most creative thinking, your full attention. The client gets a space that returns their investment in satisfaction, utility, and property value. They get back ninety-five lakhs worth of quality for their one crore. That is a return that justifies your fees a hundred times over.

If you undercharge that same client, you cut corners—staffing, time, materials, creativity. The client ends up with a crore spent and a mediocre result. And somehow, you have convinced yourself you did them a favour by charging less.

You did not. You let them down. And you let yourself down.

Entry Products, High Ticket, and Growing Your Price Over Time

I want to be honest with you about something. I am not saying you should never take low-paying work. Especially when you are starting out, or entering a new niche, there are situations where taking a smaller engagement makes sense—to build trust, demonstrate value, and establish a relationship.

This is what I call an entry product. A lower-priced, lower-scope offering that gets the client in the door and lets them experience your work before committing to a larger engagement.

The key word is entry. It is a door, not a home.

The mistake most business owners make is that they build their entire practice on entry-product pricing and never move the client—or themselves—to a higher level. They stay in the entry forever. And entry-level pricing produces entry-level revenue.

> *Your entry product should be simple, clearly scoped, and priced to cover your costs with a small margin. Its purpose is to build the relationship.*
>
> *After delivering value, the conversation should shift: 'Based on what I've seen in your business, here is a much bigger*

opportunity I can help you with—and here is what that would look like.'

High-ticket work is where your real growth comes from. One high-ticket client at premium fees will do more for your revenue and your confidence than ten low-fee clients combined.

Every year, your average ticket size should grow. If it is not growing, you are either not communicating your value clearly or not targeting clients with the budget to pay for it.

And here is something worth sitting with: premium clients are often easier to work with than budget clients. They have clearer expectations. They respect your time. They value quality over price. They pay on time. And they refer other premium clients.

Budget clients, on the other hand, often take the most time, create the most friction, negotiate hardest, and refer other budget clients.

Choose which circle you want to operate in. And price yourself into it.

How to Decide What to Charge

So how do you actually set your price? Here is a framework that works.

1. **Know the value you deliver.** Not the hours you spend—the outcome you create. What is the business result for the client? What problem are you solving? What would it cost them if this problem went unsolved? Your fee should be proportional to the value created, not the time taken.

2. **Know your market.** What are others in your niche charging? Not to copy them blindly—but to understand the range. Are you at the bottom, the middle, or the top? If you are at the bottom without a deliberate reason, that is a problem.
3. **Know your costs.** What does it actually cost you to deliver this service—staff time, overheads, your own time, tools? Your price must cover costs, pay you fairly, and leave margin to invest in growth. If it does not do all three, the price is wrong.
4. **Know your client's budget.** A client with a ten-lakh project and a client with a one-crore project are not the same client. Price accordingly. Trying to fit one standard rate across every client size is how you end up undercharging the big ones and scaring away the small ones.
5. **Test and raise.** If every single prospect you quote says yes without hesitation, your price is too low. Some rejection is healthy—it means you are pricing at a level that reflects real value. Raise your rates gradually, watch the response, and keep raising until you find the level that feels right—where clients who value quality say yes and those who only want the cheapest option self-select out.

The Stand You Need to Take

Let me come back to my construction client for a moment.

After our conversation, I asked him to look at the market honestly. Other contractors in his city were delivering comparable work—some arguably less experienced than him—at twenty to twenty-five hundred rupees per square foot. His fear of losing clients was not based on reality. It was based on a belief he had never tested.

I asked him to raise his rate to eighteen hundred rupees for his next three proposals. Not all the way to twenty-five hundred—just a step up. And to hold the line when clients pushed back, rather than immediately dropping down.

He was nervous. He was sure he would lose all three.

He converted two of them at eighteen hundred. And the one he lost was, by his own admission, the most difficult client he had ever dealt with—someone who had already argued about every line item before the project even started.

Sometimes the client you lose at a higher price is the client you should be grateful to lose.

The clients who push hardest on your price are often the ones who will push hardest on everything else. Premium pricing is a filter, not just a fee.

Decide today what your rate is. Write it down. Say it out loud until you are comfortable saying it in a client meeting without flinching. Practice the conversation. Know what you will say when the client asks for a discount.

And remember this: you are not doing your client a favour by undercharging. You are setting yourself—and them—up for a result that is less than what both of you deserve.

Charge what you are worth. Deliver what you promise. And let the quality of your work justify the price—every single time.

YOUR ACTION STEP–CHAPTER 4

This week, do a complete pricing audit of your business:

Step 1—List your current rates. Write down every service you offer and what you currently charge for it.

Step 2—Research the market. Find out what three to five competitors or peers in your niche are charging for the same or similar services. Be honest about where you sit.

Step 3—Calculate your true cost. For each service, what does it actually cost you to deliver it—staff time, your time, tools, overheads? Is your current price covering costs and leaving meaningful margin?

Step 4—Identify your underpriced services. Where is the gap between what you charge and what the market pays—or what the value you deliver justifies? Pick the one service where the gap is largest.

Step 5—Raise that price. For your next proposal or renewal, charge the higher rate. Not with apology, not with a long justification—just quote it with confidence. Note what happens.

Step 6—Write your value statement. Complete this sentence: 'When a client works with me, they get ________, which means ________, which is worth ________ to their business.' This is your answer when a client asks why your fees are higher than others.

You will not get every client at your new rate. Some will say no. That is not failure—that is filtering. The right clients, at the right price, will say yes. And those are the clients who will help you build the business you actually want.

*

Coming up in Chapter 5:

Hiring Your First Team—When to hire, who to hire first, and how to do it without burning your capital

Chapter Five

HIRING YOUR FIRST TEAM

You cannot build a business alone—and the right hire at the right time changes everything

Why I Wrote This Book–And Where That Thought Began

How many of you, as service industry owners, feel like you simply cannot find good people to work with?

If your hand went up—even mentally—this chapter is written for you.

Because I started writing this book for exactly that reason. I have multiple clients who are struggling with the same set of problems—growth, pricing, leads, systems—and I wanted to sit with all of them at once. I wanted to give each of them what I would give a close friend across a table: honest advice, real stories, and a clear direction.

But here is something I have never told anyone publicly before. The thought of helping people grow—the core belief that runs through everything I do—did not come from a book or a business course.

It came from my own staff.

A Conversation With My Brother That Changed How I Think About People

When I first started practising as a CA, I needed to hire. And like most new business owners, I struggled. Good people were not walking through the door. The ones who seemed right did not join. The ones who joined were not quite right. It was a constant, exhausting cycle.

Around that time, my brother came to me with a question. He was looking to join a CA firm and wanted my advice on where to go. Naturally, my first instinct was to bring him into my own practice. But I hesitated—and deliberately recommended other firms instead.

My reason was simple: I had seen too many families damaged by mixing business with close relationships. I did not want to risk what we had. I helped him evaluate a few good firms, had conversations with the partners, and guided him as best I could.

But during one of those conversations, I asked him something out of genuine curiosity:

"What is a person actually looking for when they choose a CA firm to join?"

His answer was not what I expected.

"I want to join a firm where I will grow. Where the work will be meaningful. Where I can see my future being built."

That was it. No mention of salary first. No mention of location or office hours. The first thing out of his mouth was growth. Future. Meaning.

And I sat with that for a long time.

Because if my own brother—someone I knew deeply, someone I cared for—was looking for these things, then every person who walked into my office looking for a job was looking for exactly the same thing. They were not just looking for a salary. They were looking for a place to build their life.

That realisation changed everything about how I think about the people who work with me.

Your Staff Are Not Employees. They Are Your Extended Family.

I do not use the word "staff" lightly, and I never think of the people who work with me as just resources on a payroll. I call them my extended family. And I mean it.

They spend eight, nine, ten hours a day in your workspace. They bring their energy, their intelligence, and their time—time they could be spending anywhere else. They are building their professional lives inside your business. That is an extraordinary act of trust.

And it comes with a responsibility on your part that too many business owners refuse to acknowledge.

> *In his landmark book 'Good to Great', Jim Collins writes about getting the right people on the bus before deciding where the bus is going. The quality of your team determines the ceiling of your business—not your technical skills, not your client list, not your brand. Your people are the business.*

The world has changed. This is not a generation that is desperate for any job at any cost. Young professionals today have options—genuine options. They can freelance, join startups, go remote, build their own practices, or choose from dozens of competing offers. If you treat them like they should be grateful to work for you, you will lose them. And losing good people is one of the most expensive things that can happen to a growing business—not just in recruitment costs, but in knowledge lost, momentum broken, and client relationships disrupted.

People do not leave companies. They leave leaders who stopped caring about their growth.

One of my best colleagues—someone who has been with me through some of the most intense periods of building the practice—once sat with me and told me why she stayed. She said: "Sir, I see my future here. I see myself growing."

That is the most powerful thing any team member can say. And when someone says it to you, it is not a compliment. It is a responsibility. It means they have bet a portion of their professional life on your ability to keep growing—and to take them with you.

Do not take that lightly.

If You Are Not Growing, You Cannot Attract People Who Want to Grow

Here is the honest truth about hiring that nobody tells you clearly enough.

The best people—the ones you actually want—will not join a stagnant business. They will join a growing one. Because growth means opportunity. It means new work, new learning, new responsibilities, new titles, new salaries.

If your business has been flat for two years, if your revenue is stuck, if your client list has not expanded, if your team of five has been the same five for three years—the signal you are sending to the talent market is: there is no future here.

And the only people who will stay in that environment are the people who have no better option.

This is why Chapters 1 through 4 had to come before this one. Because the answer to your hiring problem is not a better job posting or a higher salary offer. The answer is a growing business—one that gives talented people a reason to choose you over everyone else competing for their time.

> *Set meaningful goals and pursue them visibly—people want to be part of something with direction.*
>
> *Work in a focused niche—people want to build deep expertise, not scatter across everything.*
>
> *Generate leads consistently—people want job security, which comes from a business with a full pipeline.*
>
> *Charge premium fees—people want to work for a business they are proud of, not one that struggles to survive.*

Fix those things, and your hiring problem becomes significantly easier. Not completely solved—but easier. Because now you are a growing firm with a clear direction, interesting work, and real opportunities for advancement. That is the environment good people are looking for.

Who to Hire First–and Why Getting This Wrong is Expensive

Most business owners hire based on urgency. They are drowning in work, so they hire whoever can help them do that work. A junior version of themselves. Someone to execute the same tasks they are doing, just cheaper.

This is almost always the wrong first hire. Because it does not free you—it just adds someone to manage.

Alex Hormozi, in his book '$100M Offers', makes a point that applies powerfully here: the most valuable thing in your business is not your product or your clients—it is your time. And the first hire should be the one that gives you back the most of it.

So before you hire anyone, do one exercise. For one week, write down every task you do and how much time it takes. Then look at the list and ask: which of these tasks absolutely requires me? And which of these could someone else do—if I trained them well?

Everything in the second category is a candidate for delegation. And the person you hire first should be able to take the largest chunk of that second category off your plate.

First Hire: The Operations Person

Hire when: You are spending more than fifty percent of your time on client communication, task follow-up, file management, or internal coordination.

Why first: This frees you from the daily operational noise and gives you back the mental space to think about strategy, clients, and growth. Without this person, you will always be reactive.

Second Hire: The Specialist

Hire when: You have a niche, you have clients, and the actual delivery of your core service is consuming all your time.

Why first: This person delivers your core service—under your guidance. You shift from doing the work to reviewing and quality-checking it. Your capacity multiplies without your hours increasing.

Third Hire: The Executive Assistant

Hire when: You are spending significant time on scheduling, follow-ups, emails, reporting, and coordination that does not require your expertise.

Why first: An EA is one of the highest-leverage hires a business owner can make. Every hour you reclaim from administrative tasks is an hour that can go into strategy, client relationships, or business development.

Notice what is not on this list yet: a sales or marketing hire. That comes later—after your operations are stable enough to handle more clients. Bringing in new business before your delivery is sorted is how you damage your reputation.

Stop Working In the Business. Start Leading It.

Here is something I want to say directly, because too many business owners need to hear it.

If you are an architect and you are still drawing every plan yourself—you are not running an architecture firm. You are a freelance architect with employees.

If you are a CA and you are still filing every return personally—you are not running a practice. You are a CA with helpers.

If you are a developer and you are still writing every line of code—you are not running a tech company. You are a developer who has outsourced some tasks.

The business owner's job is not technical delivery. The business owner's job is direction, strategy, culture, and growth.

> *The biggest hospital chains in India are not run by the best doctors—they are run by administrators and business professionals who created systems for doctors to operate in. The best CA firms are not run by the most technically sound partners—they are built by people who understood how to grow a practice, attract talent, and serve clients at scale. The gap between a practitioner and a business owner is not skill. It is mindset.*

In '10X Is Easier Than 2X', Dan Sullivan and Dr. Benjamin Hardy argue that the path to exponential growth requires you to identify the twenty percent of your work that produces eighty percent of your results—and delegate everything else. The business owner who insists on doing everything themselves is not hardworking. They are, unknowingly, the biggest obstacle to their own growth.

The moment you stop being the person who does the work—and become the person who leads the work—your business starts growing without your permission.

Your job, as the owner, is three things: set the direction, build the team, and create the environment where great work can happen consistently. That is it. Everything else is a task that belongs to someone else on your team.

If you are still doing everything yourself, ask the honest question: is it because no one else can do it? Or is it because you have not taken the time to train, document, and trust someone else to do it?

Ninety percent of the time, it is the second reason.

Building a Culture That Retains Good People

Getting good people is one challenge. Keeping them is another—and in many ways, harder.

I have watched business owners invest months in finding and training a great team member, only to lose them within a year because of something that had nothing to do with salary. It was the environment. The culture. The feeling of being seen, valued, and invested in.

Here is what I have learned keeps good people:

1. **Give them growth, not just work.** Assign projects that stretch them. Give them responsibility before they are fully ready. Let them own outcomes. People who are growing do not leave.
2. **Pay them well—then pay them better.** Do not wait for someone to threaten to leave before you raise their salary. Review compensation proactively, at least annually. A well-paid team member is a loyal one.

3. **Give them visibility into the business.** Share goals. Share wins. Share challenges. People who understand what the business is trying to do feel ownership. People who are kept in the dark feel like hired hands.
4. **Freedom within structure.** Micromanagement is the fastest way to lose your best people. The best people want autonomy. Give them clear outcomes, clear standards, and then get out of the way.
5. **Recognise them publicly.** A simple acknowledgement in a team meeting—"this person did exceptional work on this"—costs nothing and means everything. People need to feel seen.

The Business That Grows While You Sleep

I want to close this chapter with an image I carry with me and share often with my clients.

Imagine two business owners, both in the same industry, both with similar clients, both with similar skills.

The first one works fourteen hours a day, handles every client personally, reviews every piece of work, answers every call, and is the single point of contact for everything. When he is on holiday, the business pauses. When he is sick, work stops. His business is built entirely around him.

The second one works six to eight hours a day, focused entirely on strategy, client relationships, and growth. Her team handles operations, delivery, and day-to-day execution. When she is on holiday, the business continues. When she is unwell, work goes on. Her business is built around systems and people.

Five years later, who has the larger, more valuable, more sustainable business?

The answer is obvious. But here is what is less obvious: the second business owner did not get there by working less. She got there by making one critical transition—from doing the work to leading the people who do the work.

That transition starts with your first hire.

Make it wisely. Make it soon. And make it with the understanding that every person you bring into your business is not just filling a role—they are becoming part of the story you are building.

Treat them accordingly.

YOUR ACTION STEP–CHAPTER 5

This week, do a complete time and team audit:

Time Audit: For five working days, write down every task you do and how long it takes. At the end of the week, mark each task: Owner Only (only you can do this) or Delegable (someone else could do this with training). Add up the hours in the Delegable column. That number tells you how much time you are leaving on the table every week.

First Hire Decision: Based on your time audit, identify the single role that would free up the most of your time if you filled it. Write a clear one-page description of what that person would do, what skills they need, and what success in that role looks like.

Growth Mirror Check: Honestly assess: is your business growing enough to attract good people? Look at your revenue trend, your client list growth, and your reputation in your niche. If the answer is no—go back to Chapters 1 through 4 and identify what needs to change first.

Culture Question: If you already have a team, ask yourself: when did I last personally acknowledge someone's good work? When did I last have a one-on-one conversation about their growth and career? Schedule one this week.

Remember: you cannot scale yourself. But you can scale a great team. Your first hire is not a cost—it is the most important investment you will ever make in your business.

*

Coming up in Chapter 6:

Building Systems and Delegating—How to stop being the bottleneck in your own business

Chapter Six

BUILDING SYSTEMS AND DELEGATING

How to stop being the most expensive operator in your own business—and finally work on it

The ₹20 Crore Man Who Had No Time

I sat down with a client of mine for what was supposed to be a two-hour annual review meeting. He had done twenty crore rupees in turnover that year. By most measures, a successful business.

But within the first ten minutes, I knew something was deeply wrong.

His phone rang. He picked up and spent three minutes directing a delivery driver on which route to take. Before he could put it down, it rang again—a vendor asking about a payment. He handled it. Another call came in—his accountant asking whether to process a supplier invoice. He answered. Then someone from his team needed approval on a quotation. Then a logistics person needed confirmation on a dispatch.

For two hours, I sat across from a man who ran a twenty-crore business—and watched him do the work of a 20,000-a-month coordinator.

At a natural pause, I said something to him that he did not take well at first.

"Sir, I know you feel busy. But you are not actually working. You are reacting."

There is a difference between being busy and being productive. Busy means your time is full. Productive means your time is creating something of value.

He pushed back immediately. "You don't understand. This is my business. I need to be on top of everything. If I step away, things fall apart."

I have heard this exact sentence from dozens of business owners. And every single time, it signals the same underlying problem: the business has no systems. And without systems, the owner becomes the system—and the business cannot grow beyond what one person can personally manage.

A twenty-crore business should not require its owner to direct a delivery driver. Ever.

Working FOR Your Business vs. Working ON Your Business

Michael Gerber, in his landmark book 'The E-Myth Revisited', describes the fatal trap that destroys most small businesses. He calls it the Technician's Trap. It goes like this:

> *A skilled person—a baker, a consultant, a contractor, an engineer—decides to start a business based on their skill. They are excellent at the technical work. So they build a business around themselves. And slowly, they become so buried in doing the technical work that they have no time to build the business. They end up with a job that is harder, longer, and less predictable than any job they could have taken working for someone else.*

This is working FOR your business. You show up every day, execute the tasks, handle the problems, fight the fires, answer the calls. The business needs you to function. Without you, it stops.

Working ON your business is different. It means you spend your time designing the machine—the processes, the team, the standards, the systems—so that the machine runs without needing you to push every gear yourself.

The business owner who works ON the business asks: how do I make this repeatable without me?

The business owner trapped working FOR the business asks: how do I get through today?

Your job is not to run every operation. Your job is to build a business that runs its own operations.

The good news: this shift does not require a large team, a big budget, or years of restructuring. It requires one thing—Standard Operating Procedures. SOPs.

What an SOP Is–And Why It Is the Most Underrated Tool in Business

An SOP—Standard Operating Procedure—is simply a written description of how a task should be done, every time, by anyone.

That is it. No fancy software needed. No management consultant required. Just a clear, written answer to the question: how do we do this?

In my own practice, we handle over eighty GST returns every month. When I started, every return was managed personally by me—or with very heavy supervision. It consumed hours I did not have. If I was travelling or unwell, the work piled up.

Then we built an SOP for GST return filing. Step by step—how data is collected from the client, how it is entered, how it is reviewed, how the return is filed, how confirmation is sent. Every step documented. Every responsibility assigned.

Today, my team handles all eighty-plus returns. I review the output once. The machine runs without me pushing every part of it.

That is the power of an SOP. Not just efficiency—freedom.

The Half-Hour Payment System–How We Fixed My Client's Biggest Time Drain

Let me go back to my twenty-crore client and the payment problem specifically, because it is such a perfect example of how a simple system eliminates a massive time drain.

Before our conversation, here is how his payment process worked:

- *A vendor would call asking when their payment was due.*
- *My client would try to remember the invoice, check his phone, think about cash flow, and give a verbal answer.*
- *The vendor would call again a few days later to follow up.*
- *My client would be in a meeting, miss the call, call back later, forget again.*
- *Eventually, under pressure, he would call his accountant and ask for a check—sometimes urgently, sometimes late.*
- *The whole cycle consumed multiple calls, interruptions, and mental energy every single week.*

Here is what we replaced it with:

Step 1—Monthly projected cash flow: At the start of every month, the accountant prepares a list of all vendor payments due in the next thirty to forty-five days, with exact dates and amounts. This sits in a shared file.

Step 2—Weekly payment batch: Every week—same day, same time—the accountant compiles that week's due payments into one document with the purchase invoice, delivery receipt, and payment details attached.

Step 3—Owner review: thirty minutes maximum: My client sits with this document once a week. He reviews, approves, and signs. That is it. Thirty minutes. One sitting. No calls, no follow-ups, no interruptions.

Step 4—Execution: The accountant processes all approved payments. Vendors are notified. Done.

The result: an activity that was consuming hours of interrupted, scattered attention every week was compressed into thirty focused minutes. The vendors got paid on time. The stress disappeared. And my client had his afternoons back.

He looked at me after we mapped this out and said: "This sounds too simple. Why have I not been doing this already?"

That is always the reaction. Systems sound obvious in hindsight. The reason people do not build them is not complexity—it is that they are too busy reacting to invest even a few hours in designing a better way.

> *Ray Dalio, founder of the world's largest hedge fund Bridgewater Associates, built his entire organisation on one principle: document everything into principles and processes so that the right decision can be made every time—with or without him in the room. He describes this in his book 'Principles'. The scale is different, but the idea applies to a twenty-crore business just as powerfully as it does to a two-hundred-billion-dollar fund.*

How to Build Your First SOPs–Start Small, Start Now

You do not need to document your entire business in one weekend. You need to start with the tasks that consume the most of your time or cause the most problems when they go wrong.

Here is a simple framework for building your first set of SOPs:

1. **Identify your top five time drains.** Which tasks are you personally doing that happen repeatedly—daily, weekly, or monthly? Payments, client follow-ups, team briefings, quotation approvals, report preparation? List them.

2. **Document how it is done today.** For each task, write down every step—exactly as it currently happens. Do not aim for perfect. Aim for accurate. A rough SOP is infinitely more useful than no SOP.
3. **Identify who could do this instead of you.** Is there a team member who could own this task if they had the written process in front of them? If yes, that person is your first delegate.
4. **Train once, then let go.** Walk the person through the SOP once. Let them try it. Review the output. Give feedback. Adjust the SOP if needed. Then step back and let them own it.
5. **Build in a review checkpoint, not daily interference.** Do not micromanage the process. Instead, schedule a brief weekly or fortnightly review: is this happening correctly? Are the outputs right? That is your involvement—not daily hand-holding.

Think about the companies you admire most—the ones operating at hundreds or thousands of crores of revenue. They have SOPs for everything. Not because they are large, but because they understood early that scale is impossible without standardisation. They did not wait until they were big to build systems. They built systems to become big.

If you want to operate at a hundred crore, you must start building like a hundred-crore company today—even if you are at two crore. The systems you build now are the foundation everything else is built on.

The Most Important Meeting You Are Not Having–With Yourself

There is one more practice I want to introduce in this chapter—one that sounds almost too simple to be transformational. But I have seen it change the trajectory of businesses when it is taken seriously.

Every week, you must schedule three to four hours of uninterrupted time to work ON your business.

Not with clients. Not in operations. Not on calls or approvals or payments.

Alone. With your numbers, your plans, your team review, and your thinking.

Call it your CEO Block. Your Strategy Hour. Your Business Review. Whatever name makes it sacred to you. The name does not matter. The practice does.

The business that gets three hours of your strategic thinking every week will outgrow the business that gets zero—no matter how hard you work in the remaining hours.

Here is what those three to four hours should cover:

- **Revenue review:** What came in this week? How does it compare to last week and to your monthly target? Where are you ahead or behind?
- **Lead and pipeline review:** How many new conversations happened? How many proposals are open? What follow-ups are overdue?

- **Team pulse:** Is everyone clear on their priorities? Is anyone stuck? Is any process breaking down? Where does someone need support or a decision from you?
- **Operations health check:** Are the SOPs running smoothly? Were there any fires this week that a better system could have prevented?
- **Strategic priorities:** What are the two or three things that, if you moved them forward this week, would have the biggest impact on growth? Did you make progress on them?
- **Personal energy:** Are you working on the right things? Are you drifting back into operational work? Do you need to delegate something new?

This block is not optional. It is not something you do when you have time—because you will never have time if you do not protect it. Put it in your calendar right now. Same day, same time, every week. Guard it like your most important client meeting.

Because it is, in fact, the most important meeting you will ever have.

What Happened to My Twenty-Crore Client

I want to close this chapter by coming back to where we started—the man whose phone would not stop ringing.

After our two-hour session, he was still sceptical. But he agreed to try three things: the weekly payment batching system, a dedicated coordinator for delivery follow-ups, and a Friday afternoon CEO Block for himself.

Within six weeks, he called me.

"My phone has stopped ringing," he said.

He sounded almost surprised. As if the silence was unfamiliar. As if he had forgotten that business could feel like this.

"Now what do I do with the time?" he asked.

"Now," I told him, "you grow."

He used that reclaimed time to meet three new potential clients he had been too busy to call. He signed two of them. His monthly revenue grew by fifteen percent in a quarter—not because the market changed, not because he worked harder, but because he finally had the time and mental clarity to work on his business instead of inside it.

That is what systems do. They do not just save time. They create the space where growth becomes possible.

YOUR ACTION STEP–CHAPTER 6

This week, three things—no postponing:

The Five-Task List: Write down the five tasks you personally do most often that could theoretically be done by someone else with the right instructions. For each one, estimate how many hours per week it consumes. Add it up. That is your freedom number—the hours you will reclaim when you build systems for these tasks.

Build One SOP: Choose the single most time-consuming task from your list. Today, write a simple step-by-step process for how it should be done. It does not need to be perfect—two pages, clear steps, clear ownership. That is your first SOP. Hand it to a team member and brief them on it this week.

Book Your CEO Block: Open your calendar right now. Block three to four hours this week—and every week going forward—for your business review. Label it something that makes it feel non-negotiable. No client calls. No operations. Just you and your business.

A business that runs without you is not a dream. It is a design decision. Start designing it this week.

*

Coming up in Chapter 7:

The Growth Engine—How reputation, referrals, and revenue compound when you do the right things consistently

Chapter Seven

THE GROWTH ENGINE

How reputation, content, and consistent visibility create a flywheel that generates business—without you chasing it

The Meeting Where No Introduction Was Needed

A lead came in—one of Pune's well-known companies, solid reputation, respected brand. When I reached out, they invited me for a meeting.

I walked in and sat down. The decision-maker across the table got straight to the point.

"I have gone through your Instagram and YouTube. I know who you are and what you do. I do not need you to pitch yourself. Just tell me what you can specifically do for me—and we can move forward."

The meeting I had expected to spend building trust, explaining credentials, and establishing credibility was already past all of that before it began.

That is what consistent, long-term content does. It does the selling before you enter the room.

The best sales meeting is the one where the client already trusts you before you say your first word.

That moment did not happen by accident. It was the result of years of consistent content—videos, posts, insights—that I had been putting out since 2019. And when I started, let me tell you what happened.

2019: When People Laughed

In 2019, I started making videos. Short educational content on GST, business growth, compliance—the things I knew well. I posted them on Instagram. I put some on YouTube. I showed up consistently, talking to a camera, sharing what I knew.

And people laughed.

Not openly or cruelly—but in the way that people from conservative professional backgrounds react when someone does something that feels out of place. "Why is a CA making videos?" "Who does he think he is?" "This is not serious work."

The background most of us come from does not celebrate visibility. Being vocal about your expertise, putting yourself in front of a camera, creating content for the public—it feels uncomfortable. It feels vulnerable. And in some circles, it is quietly judged.

I understood that discomfort. I felt it myself. But I had a longer view. And I kept going.

Gary Vaynerchuk, one of the most influential voices on business and content, has argued for years that we are living in the greatest era of opportunity for individuals to build their own media—for free. The tools that previously required crores in advertising budgets are now available to anyone with a smartphone. The only cost is consistency and the willingness to show up.

Today, the same people who laughed are asking me how to start their own content. Today, a top Pune company invites me in because they already know me through a screen. Today, referrals come from people who have never met me personally but have been watching my content for two years.

The world moved. The ones who moved with it are compounding. The ones who waited are still wondering why business is not coming.

Stop Being a Consumer. Become a Provider.

Here is the most important reframe I can give you about social media.

Most business owners use it as consumers. They scroll, watch, and spend four to five hours a day absorbing content that other people created. At the end of it they close the app feeling vaguely entertained—and no closer to their goals.

The business owners who are winning are on the same apps—but as providers. They are the ones creating the content others are consuming. And the difference in outcome between these two groups is not small. It is enormous.

Every hour you spend consuming content is an hour someone else uses to build their reputation. Choose which side of the screen you want to be on.

People in India spend more than four to five hours a day on their phones. A significant portion of that is on WhatsApp, Instagram, YouTube, and LinkedIn. Your potential clients are there. Your referral sources are there. The question is not whether social media works—it does. The question is whether you are showing up, or hiding.

And the bar for showing up is far lower than you think.

5,000 Followers–Bigger Than You Realise

I want to tell you about a client of mine in the construction business. He started posting videos six months ago. Short clips—project updates, construction tips, site walk-throughs, quick insights on material quality and costing. Nothing elaborate. Shot on a phone. Posted consistently.

He has built a following of over five thousand people.

When I mentioned it as a milestone, he shrugged. "It is not much," he said.

I stopped him.

"Close your eyes. Imagine you have rented an auditorium. Five thousand people are sitting in front of you. You walk on stage and speak about your work, your expertise, your projects. How does that feel?"

He was quiet.

"That is your audience," I said. "Five thousand people who chose to follow you. Who have seen your face, your work, your values. When any one of them—or anyone they know—needs a construction contractor, whose name comes to mind first?"

5,000 followers is not a small number. It is a stadium full of people who know your name and have seen your work.

You do not need a million followers to win business. You need the right five hundred, one thousand, two thousand people—your niche audience—to know, like, and trust you. Out of every two hundred people watching your content, even if just one or two become clients or refer clients, that compounds over months and years into a self-sustaining pipeline.

That is a growth engine.

What Marketing Actually Is–And What It Is Not

Marketing is not advertising. It is not spending money on Meta campaigns, Google ads, or expensive brand photoshoots. Those tools have their place—but they are for later, when you have revenue to invest and a clear message to amplify.

For your first crore, marketing is reputation.

Reputation is what people say about you when you are not in the room. In the digital age, your content is the room. Every post, every video, every insight you share is a brick in the structure of your reputation. Over time, that structure becomes unmissable.

- *When you post a client success story, you tell the market: I deliver results.*
- *When you share an insight about your industry, you tell the market: I know my field deeply.*
- *When you show up consistently for a year, you tell the market: I am reliable.*
- *When someone searches your name before a meeting and finds two years of valuable content, the trust is already there before you walk in.*

This is not about vanity or follower counts as ego metrics. It is about building a digital track record that does your selling, your trust-building, and your reputation management—automatically, continuously, and for free.

As Seth Godin puts it: marketing is no longer about the stuff you make but the stories you tell. Your content is your story. Start telling it.

The Referral Flywheel–How Reputation Compounds Into Revenue

Here is how the full growth engine works when all the pieces are in place. Think of it as a flywheel—once it starts spinning, every rotation makes the next one easier.

1. You post consistently—knowledge, insights, client results, your perspective.
2. Your existing network sees your content. They remember you. They trust you more deeply.
3. When someone in their circle needs your service, your name comes up naturally.

4. The referred person looks you up. They find months of content. Trust is already built.
5. The first meeting is not a pitch—it is a conversation between two people who feel they already know each other.
6. You convert. You deliver great work. The new client becomes part of your story.
7. Their network sees this. The flywheel spins faster. Referrals multiply.

This is exactly what happened with my Pune client. He found me through content. He arrived with trust already built. We closed quickly. He has since referred three other businesses. One piece of content, consistently amplified over years, is worth more than a one-time advertising campaign that costs ten times as much. Because content compounds. Advertising stops when you stop paying.

What to Post, Where to Post, and How Often

Let me make this practical. You do not need a content agency or a video production team. You need a phone, fifteen minutes a day, and something genuine to say about the work you do.

WhatsApp Status and Broadcast

Post: Short insights, client wins, quick tips related to your niche. One to two updates daily.

Key insight: Your existing contacts are already here. This is your warmest audience. Start here first—before any other platform.

Instagram Reels and Posts

Post: Short videos explaining one concept, one result, one insight. Behind-the-scenes of your work. Two to three times a week.

Key insight: Reels get discovered by people outside your network. Best for building new niche audience over time.

LinkedIn

Post: Written posts sharing business lessons, client observations, industry insights, your professional journey. Two to three times a week.

Key insight: Best platform for B2B service businesses. Decision-makers are active here. High quality engagement from the right audience.

YouTube

Post: Longer videos of five to fifteen minutes explaining complex topics in depth. Once a week or fortnightly.

Key insight: YouTube is the second largest search engine. A video you post today can generate leads two years from now. Long shelf life.

Do not try to be everywhere at once. Start with one platform—the one where your ideal clients spend the most time. Build the habit. Then expand.

The most common question I get: what should I talk about? Talk about what you know. The problems your clients face. Mistakes you see businesses make. What you wish more people understood about your industry. Your client successes. Your own journey.

You do not need to be a polished communicator. You need to be genuine. In a world full of produced, artificial content—genuine is rare. And rare is remembered.

This Is a Long Game–Play It Like One

I want to be honest with you, because pretending otherwise would be a disservice.

Content marketing does not produce results in thirty days. It produces results in six months, twelve months, two years. The compounding happens slowly at first—and then suddenly, dramatically.

Most people quit at month two because they posted fifteen times and saw no visible results. They declare it does not work and go back to reactive, hope-based business development.

The people who stay—who post through the months when no one seems to be watching, who show up even when engagement is low, who keep sharing their knowledge even when it feels like shouting into a void—those are the people who receive a call from a company two years later saying: "I have been following your content. I already know what you do. Let us talk."

Six months of consistent content will do more for your business than the most expensive marketing campaign money can buy.

The construction client with five thousand followers did not get there in a week. He got there by posting for six months—through weeks when his videos got forty views, through months when engagement dipped, through days when he was tired but posted anyway.

Now those five thousand people are his warmest pipeline. Built for free. Built through consistency. Built to last.

Start today. Post something. It does not need to be perfect. It needs to be honest, useful, and in your voice.

Because somewhere out there, your next best client is scrolling right now—looking for someone who knows what you know, does what you do, and shows up consistently enough to earn their trust.

Make sure they find you.

YOUR ACTION STEP–CHAPTER 7

This week—start. Not plan to start. Actually start.

Choose your one platform: Where do your ideal clients spend time? Pick one—WhatsApp, Instagram, or LinkedIn. Just one. Build the habit first, expand later.

Post this week: One video, one written post, one insight from your work this week. No editing required. No perfection required. Just post.

Commit to a content schedule: Write it down: I will post ___ times per week on ___. Block fifteen minutes daily. Treat it as a non-negotiable client commitment.

Audit your profiles: Make sure your Instagram, LinkedIn, and WhatsApp Business profile clearly says who you are, who you serve, and what you do. A strong profile converts viewers into followers and followers into enquiries.

Set a three-month reminder: Mark your calendar ninety days from today. On that date, review everything you have posted. You will surprise yourself—and the momentum will carry you forward.

The people who laugh at you today for posting will call you for advice two years from now. Keep going.

*

Coming up in Chapter 8:

Profit Over Turnover—Why the number that matters most is not your revenue, and how to protect it

Chapter Eight

PROFIT OVER TURNOVER

The number that impresses others is not the number that changes your life—and here is how to protect the one that does

The Question That Reveals Everything

At every business gathering, every networking event, every casual conversation between entrepreneurs, there is one question that comes up almost immediately.

"What is your turnover?"

Not: what is your profit? Not: how much did you take home last year? Not: is your business growing in a way that is actually making your life better?

Turnover. Revenue. The top line.

And I understand why. Turnover is visible. It sounds impressive. It is easy to say and easy to compare. A person doing five crore turnover sounds, on the surface, like they are in a different league from someone doing one crore.

But here is the question I have started asking in those same rooms, when the turnover conversation comes up:

"Interesting. And what was your profit?"

The silence that follows is always instructive.

Turnover tells you how much passed through your hands. Profit tells you how much you actually kept. Only one of those numbers changes your life.

I have sat with business owners doing eight crore, ten crore, even fifteen crore in annual turnover—who were taking home less net profit than a salaried professional working for someone else. All that revenue, all that effort, all that risk—and the owner's real income was a fraction of what the top line suggested.

This chapter is about flipping the obsession. From revenue to profit. From the number that impresses people at dinner parties to the number that actually builds wealth, freedom, and a future.

Busy, Successful–and Broke on Paper

A client of mine—a service business owner—came to me one year very proud of his revenue. He had crossed five crore in turnover for the first time. He had celebrated. His team had celebrated. He posted about it.

When we sat down and went through his accounts properly, the picture changed.

His direct costs of service delivery—staff salaries, subcontractors, tools—were eating sixty percent of revenue. His office rent, utilities, and overheads took another fifteen percent. Marketing spends, software subscriptions, and miscellaneous costs took another ten percent. Loan repayments and interest took five percent more.

At the end of it, his actual net profit was less than ten percent of his revenue. On five crore turnover, he was keeping less than fifty lakh rupees.

Not a bad number in isolation. But for the stress, the team, the risk, and the years of effort that went into building a five-crore business—it was underwhelming. And crucially, he had no clear picture of where that fifty lakh was going, no plan for how to grow it, and no understanding of which parts of his business were profitable and which were quietly bleeding money.

> *Warren Buffett, arguably the greatest investor in history, has one simple principle he returns to again and again: revenue is vanity, profit is sanity, and cash flow is reality. A business that generates impressive revenue but produces no sustainable profit is not a business—it is an expensive hobby.*

The moment we laid out his real numbers—line by line—he saw things he had never seen before. Two service lines that looked like winners were actually loss-making when you factored in the true cost of delivery. One client segment that he had considered small was generating the highest margins in the business. Two team members whose salaries were justified by their revenue contribution—and three whose cost was not being recovered by the work they produced.

That single session—looking honestly at profit, not turnover—produced more strategic clarity than three years of running on instinct.

Why Tracking Profit Is Not an Accounting Exercise–It Is a Survival Skill

Let me be very direct here. Many business owners treat profit tracking as something that happens after the fact—something their accountant does at year-end for tax purposes. They run the business on feel, on cash flow appearances, on whatever is in the current account.

This is one of the most dangerous ways to run a business.

Because cash in your account is not profit. Revenue deposits are not profit. A busy calendar is not profit. A growing client list is not profit.

Profit is what remains after every cost has been paid—and it is the only true measure of whether your business is sustainable.

- *A business with high revenue and low profit is fragile—one bad month, one lost client, one unexpected cost can tip it into loss.*
- *A business with moderate revenue and healthy profit is resilient—it can absorb shocks, invest in growth, and reward its owner consistently.*
- *A business that tracks profit monthly can course-correct early—before a margin problem becomes a cash flow crisis.*
- *A business that only looks at the numbers once a year is always surprised—and surprises in business are almost never good ones.*

Tracking profit regularly—monthly, at minimum—is not bureaucracy. It is the instrument panel of your business. It tells you whether you are flying level, climbing, or heading toward the ground. And unlike the dashboard of a plane, you can only read it if you build it deliberately.

You cannot manage what you do not measure. And you cannot grow what you cannot manage.

What to Track–The Numbers Every Business Owner Must Know

You do not need to be a finance expert to track your business's health. You need to understand five numbers—and review them every single month.

Revenue—Total money billed and collected from clients this month. *(Your starting point—not your destination.)*

Direct Costs—The cost of delivering your service—staff, materials, subcontractors, tools directly tied to projects. *(The first and most important deduction. This gives you Gross Profit.)*

Gross Profit and Gross Margin—Revenue minus Direct Costs, expressed as a percentage of Revenue. *(Your business's true earning power before overheads. Below 40% in most service businesses is a warning sign.)*

Overheads—Rent, utilities, non-project salaries, software, marketing, loan repayments—costs that exist regardless of how much work you do. *(These must be covered by Gross Profit. If they are not, you are loss-making at the operating level.)*

Net Profit and Net Margin—Gross Profit minus Overheads. This is what you actually made. *(The number that matters. For service businesses, a healthy net margin is fifteen to thirty percent. Below ten percent needs urgent attention.)*

Once you know these five numbers every month, patterns become visible that are invisible when you are just watching the current account. You see which months are strong and which are weak. You see when overheads are creeping up faster than revenue. You see when gross margins are shrinking—often the earliest warning sign of a pricing or cost problem.

And most importantly, you can act—before problems become crises.

The Revenue Obsession–Why It Leads You Astray

Here is something worth sitting with.

When you chase revenue—when the goal is to grow the top line—you make certain kinds of decisions. You take on more clients, even at lower margins. You add more services, even if you are not set up to deliver them profitably. You hire more people to handle more work, without checking whether the economics of that work justify the cost.

You get busier. Your business gets bigger. Your team gets larger. And your profit, paradoxically, stays flat or shrinks—because every new rupee of revenue came with costs that ate most of it.

When you chase profit—when the goal is to protect and grow the bottom line—you make completely different decisions.

Client selection: Take every client who will pay **vs** Filter for clients with the best margin profile

Pricing: Price to win, drop to close **vs** Price on value, hold the line

New services: Add anything the market will buy **vs** Only add services that meet margin targets

Hiring: Hire when you feel busy **vs** Hire when numbers justify the cost

Expenses: Spend when cash is available **vs** Spend only when ROI is clear

The profit-focused business owner is not less ambitious than the revenue-focused one. They are more disciplined. And in the long run, the disciplined business is the one that survives, scales, and creates real wealth for its owner.

A business that does two crore in revenue and keeps forty lakh in profit is stronger than one that does five crore and keeps the same forty lakh. Always choose the cleaner business.

How to Actually Improve Your Profit–Three Levers

Profit improvement is not complicated. There are exactly three ways to do it, and every strategy in this book connects to at least one of them.

1. **Increase revenue without increasing costs proportionally.** This is the power of pricing correctly—Chapter 4—and generating better leads—Chapter 3. When you raise your fees or bring in higher-value clients, revenue grows without your cost base growing at the same rate. The extra revenue drops almost directly to the bottom line.

2. **Reduce direct costs without reducing quality.** Look hard at how you deliver your service. Are there inefficiencies in your process? Are you over-staffed for the revenue you are generating? Are subcontractors or suppliers charging more than the market rate? Chapter 6—systems and SOPs—is fundamentally a profit improvement tool, because efficient delivery costs less.
3. **Reduce overheads that are not generating returns.** Every expense in your business should earn its place. Review your overhead line every quarter. Which expenses directly contribute to revenue or client retention? Which are habits or conveniences that you have never questioned? The ones with no clear return are candidates for reduction or elimination.

Most business owners, when they want to improve profit, focus only on the first lever—they try to sell more. But often the fastest wins are in the second and third levers—costs that can be tightened without any impact on client experience or team morale.

Do all three systematically, and your profit will improve significantly within one financial year—often without your revenue growing at all.

Withdrawing Profit–The Part Nobody Talks About

There is one aspect of profit that business owners almost never discuss openly, and it is the part that matters most to the actual quality of your life.

Taking it out.

Many business owners who do generate good profit leave it sitting in the business—reinvesting everything, paying themselves the minimum, deferring personal financial security indefinitely in the belief that every rupee should go back into growth.

To a point, this is wise. Reinvestment is how businesses compound. But taken too far, it creates a business owner who has built genuine value on paper but has no personal financial security, no investments outside the business, and no ability to weather a personal crisis without putting the business at risk.

The goal of building a business is ultimately personal freedom and security. If the business is growing but the owner's personal financial life is not improving, something has gone wrong.

- *Pay yourself a proper salary—not the minimum you can survive on, but a salary that reflects the value you bring to the business.*
- *When profit is strong, declare a dividend or owner's withdrawal. This is your return on the risk you have taken.*
- *Build a personal financial cushion outside the business—fixed deposits, mutual funds, property—so that your personal life is not entirely dependent on the business's fortunes.*
- *Reinvest what remains in the business thoughtfully—in people, systems, and growth initiatives with clear returns.*

The one crore profit milestone that this book is built around is not just a business metric. It is the point at which the owner can pay themselves very well, reinvest meaningfully in growth, and begin building personal wealth outside the business—all simultaneously.

That is real financial freedom. And profit tracking is the only road that leads there.

The Monthly Profit Review–Your Most Important Business Ritual

Everything I have described in this chapter requires one habit to make it real: a monthly profit review. No exceptions. No postponements. No "I will look at it when tax time comes."

On the same date every month—I recommend the fifth or tenth—sit with your P&L. It does not need to take more than an hour. But it must happen every month, every year, without fail.

Ask yourself these questions every time:

- Was this month's revenue higher or lower than last month? Why?
- Was gross margin better or worse than last month? What changed?
- Which service line or client segment was most profitable this month?
- Which was least profitable—or loss-making?
- Are overheads growing faster than revenue? If yes, where?
- What is my net profit for the month, and is it on track toward my annual target from Chapter 1?
- What is one thing I will do differently next month based on what I see today?

That last question is the most important one. Because the monthly review is not a reporting exercise—it is a decision-making exercise. The numbers tell you a story. Your job is to listen to the story and make one better decision because of it.

Over twelve months, twelve better decisions—made with full information, every single month—will produce a business that looks radically different from the one that made twelve reactive decisions based on gut feel and cash flow appearances.

Reviewing your profit monthly is not finance. It is respect—for your work, your risk, and your future.

From Revenue Pride to Profit Peace

I want to leave you with one final image for this chapter.

There are two business owners. Both work hard. Both have good client relationships. Both have been in business for about five years.

The first one talks about turnover. He knows his revenue number to the rupee and shares it freely. His profit, he is less certain about—he has a rough idea, but the details are handled by his accountant and he looks at them once a year.

The second one talks about margins. She knows her gross margin, her net margin, and her profit this month, last month, and compared to the same month last year. She knows which clients make her the most money and which cost more than they return. She withdraws a healthy salary every month and has started investing outside the business.

Five years from now, who has built more wealth?

The answer is obvious. And the only difference between them is not talent, not market, not luck. It is attention. The second owner pays attention to the right number.

Start paying attention to the right number.

YOUR ACTION STEP–CHAPTER 8

This month, take full ownership of your profit number:

Build your P&L: If you do not have a monthly Profit and Loss statement, create one this week. Revenue, direct costs, gross profit, overheads, net profit. Five numbers. One page. Ask your accountant to help if needed—but make sure you understand every line yourself.

Calculate your net margin: Divide your net profit by your total revenue and multiply by 100. That is your net margin percentage. If it is below 15%, you have a margin problem that needs urgent attention. If it is above 25%, you are doing well—now protect it.

Identify your most and least profitable work: Look at your client list or service lines. Which ones have the best gross margin? Which consume the most cost relative to revenue? Make a decision about at least one low-margin engagement—raise the price, renegotiate, or plan an exit.

Set a monthly review date: Pick a date—the 5th or 10th of every month. Block two hours. This is your monthly profit review. It starts this month. No exceptions.

Decide your owner's withdrawal: What should you be paying yourself every month? Write the number down. If your current salary is significantly below that number, identify what profit target the business needs to hit to make it possible—and connect it to your goal from Chapter 1.

Turnover is the story you tell at networking events. Profit is the story you tell yourself when the room is quiet. Make it a story worth telling.

*

Coming up in Chapter 9

Compliance as a Foundation—Why getting your legal and financial house in order is not a burden—it is a competitive advantage

Chapter Nine

THE RULES ARE NOT OPTIONAL

Why compliance is not a cost, not a burden, and not your CA's problem—it is the foundation your entire future is built on

The Man Who Built on Sand

Imagine a man who opens a tea stall on a piece of land he does not own. No agreement, no paperwork, no permission. The stall does well. Business is good. Customers love his chai. He expands—adds a few tables, puts up a proper shed, hires two people.

For three years, he runs a thriving little business.

Then one morning, the actual owner of the land shows up with a municipal notice. The stall is illegal. It must be dismantled within seven days.

Three years of work. Gone in a notice.

The tragedy is not that he was unlucky. The tragedy is that the foundation was always wrong—and he knew it. He just assumed the problem would never come. He assumed that as long as business was good, the paperwork did not matter.

This is what ignoring compliance looks like. Not a small technical error. A foundation of sand that holds the business up right until it does not.

You can build a beautiful business on weak foundations. But you cannot keep it there for long.

I have had this conversation—in different forms—with hundreds of business owners over the years. And every single time, compliance comes up, the reaction is the same.

"Why do we need to pay so much tax? The government is taking money from my pocket. India is too expensive for business."

I listen. I understand the frustration. And then I say something that usually changes the conversation.

A Different Way to Look at Taxes

Here is a thought I want you to sit with.

You are running a business in India. Your clients are in India. The roads your delivery person drives on are in India. The electricity powering your office is an Indian infrastructure project. The education system that trained your employees was Indian. The legal framework that allows you to sign contracts, own property, and sue for non-payment—Indian.

Every rupee of tax you pay is a contribution to the ecosystem that makes your business possible. Without it—without development, without infrastructure, without a functioning state—there is no market. No buyers. No business.

Paying taxes is not a cost. It is a membership fee for the market you are profiting from. Pay it with pride—and plan it with intelligence.

Now. Having said that—there is a crucial distinction I make with every client, every time this conversation comes up. And it is the most important sentence in this chapter.

There is a very thin line between tax evasion and tax planning. One is illegal and will eventually destroy your business. The other is intelligent, legal, and is what every smart business owner should be doing.

Tax evasion: hiding income, not filing returns, collecting GST from clients and pocketing it, paying employees off the books. This is a crime. And in India, the GST system, the TDS framework, and digital banking have made it increasingly impossible to hide.

Tax planning: legally structuring your business, income, and expenses to minimise the tax you owe—within the full boundaries of the law. This is not just allowed. It is smart.

Most business owners who complain about taxes are not doing tax planning. They are doing nothing—and then reacting in shock when the bill arrives.

Story One: The Contractor and the 18% Shock

I was sitting with a client who runs a civil contracting business. Young guy, ambitious, growing fast. He had been getting work from a few medium-sized developers and was doing a decent volume of business.

Then one day he called me, completely shaken.

"Sir, my client is refusing to pay me GST. He says his company is claiming input credit so there is no problem. But I am registered for GST. I have to pay eighteen percent to the government. My margin on this project is only twelve percent. If I pay GST out of my pocket, I am working at a loss."

He was right to be worried. And the situation he was in is one of the most common traps I see small service and construction businesses fall into—particularly when they are starting out.

Here is what I told him.

"You are thinking about this from the wrong end. The question is not how to avoid paying GST—the question is how to restructure your registration so that your GST burden is manageable given your margins."

I explained to him: the Composition Scheme.

> *The Composition Scheme is one of the most underutilised tools available to small Indian businesses. Under this scheme, a service business with annual turnover up to fifty lakh rupees pays GST at only six percent of turnover—instead of the standard eighteen percent. A trading business with turnover up to one point five crore pays only one percent. The trade-off: you cannot claim input tax credit, and you cannot charge GST to your clients. But for many small businesses where clients are not claiming input credit anyway, this is a dramatically better deal.*

My contractor client's situation was perfect for this. His clients were individual developers and small builders—none of whom were claiming GST input. His turnover was below the threshold. We restructured his registration, moved him to the Composition Scheme, and his GST burden dropped from eighteen percent of billing to six percent of turnover.

Same business. Same clients. Same work. Less than half the GST cost.

This is tax planning. Not evasion. Not avoidance. Legal, intelligent, fully within the system—and saving him lakhs every year.

The Real Cost of Ignoring Compliance–What Nobody Calculates

Let me now talk about the other side of the coin. Because tax planning is only half the story. The other half is filing on time, every time—and understanding what happens when you do not.

Most business owners think of compliance as a nuisance. A distraction. Something to deal with when there is time. And so they delay, defer, forget, and push things to the last minute.

What they never calculate is the actual rupee cost of non-compliance. Let me show you.

- ⚠ **GST late filing penalty:** ₹100 per day per return. Two returns per month (GSTR-1 and GSTR-3B) means ₹200 per day. Over six months of delay—₹36,000 in penalties. Just for being late.
- ⚠ **Income tax late payment interest:** If you pay your advance tax or final tax late, the government charges 12% per annum interest on the unpaid amount. Pay after the deadline and it goes to 24% in some cases.

- ⚠ **TDS non-deduction or late deposit:** Interest of 1.5% per month from the date of deduction. Penalty up to the amount of TDS not deducted. And the expense itself may be disallowed—meaning you pay tax on income you already spent.
- ⚠ **Provident Fund and ESI non-compliance:** Penalties, interest, and in serious cases—criminal liability for the business owner personally. Not just a fine. Potential prosecution.
- ⚠ **GST demand with interest:** If GST collected from clients is not deposited to the government, interest at 18 to 24% applies from the date it was due. On large amounts, this can dwarf the original tax itself.

  One business owner I worked with had deferred his GST filing for eight months. The returns he had to file late came with penalties, interest on unpaid tax, and the loss of input tax credit he could have claimed but cannot claim retroactively beyond a certain period. His total avoidable cost: over four lakh rupees. His CA's annual fee: forty thousand rupees. He had tried to save the forty thousand—and paid four lakh.

This is not a hypothetical. I have seen versions of this story dozens of times. The business owner who avoided the CA's fee to save money—and paid ten times that amount in penalties, interest, and legal costs.

Compliance is not expensive. Non-compliance is expensive. The difference is that compliance costs are predictable and manageable. Non-compliance costs arrive as emergencies.

Story Two: The Loan That Never Came

A manufacturing client of mine had been building his business steadily for six years. By the time I met him, he was doing close to eight crore in annual turnover. Good products, solid client base, a team of twenty-five. He had reached the point where he needed a significant capital injection—a working capital loan of one crore to fund a new production line that would take him to fifteen crore.

He went to the bank with confidence. He had receipts. He had invoices. He had bank statements showing a healthy volume of transactions.

The bank asked for three years of audited financial statements, GST returns, income tax returns, and TDS compliance records.

He went quiet.

His GST returns were partially filed—some months were missing. Two years of income tax returns were not filed because "the CA had not completed them." His TDS was partially deducted and partially deposited. His books had not been properly audited.

The loan was rejected.

Not because his business was bad. Not because his revenue was insufficient. But because on paper—the only paper that matters to a banker—his business did not exist cleanly. There were gaps, inconsistencies, and unanswered questions that no banker is willing to take a risk on.

Your compliance record is your business's credit score. It tells the world whether you can be trusted with other people's money.

It took us fourteen months to clean up his records—filing missing returns, getting audits done, resolving TDS discrepancies. Fourteen months of corrective work that could have been avoided entirely by simply staying current on compliance from day one.

He got the loan eventually. But he lost fourteen months of growth. A new production line that could have been running for over a year was delayed—and the revenue it would have generated was simply gone.

The cost of that delay was far greater than any CA fee he might have paid over those six years.

Story Three: The Investor Who Asked One Question

This one is shorter—but it is perhaps the most instructive of all.

A young entrepreneur I know had built a genuinely exciting business. A SaaS product for the logistics sector, growing well, with two or three marquee clients already signed. He had pitched to a venture capital firm and they were genuinely interested. Due diligence had begun.

The VC's team asked for the standard package—incorporation documents, shareholding pattern, financial statements, GST and income tax compliance records.

Within two days, the VC sent a polite but firm email. They were stepping back from the investment.

Their reason: the company had not filed its annual returns with the Registrar of Companies for two years. Its income tax filing was eighteen months overdue. One of the director's DIN—Director Identification Number—had been flagged as inactive due to non-compliance.

The business model was not the problem. The product was not the problem. The growth was not the problem.

The compliance record was the problem. And for a sophisticated investor who needs to show their own investors a clean, auditable portfolio company—no amount of revenue growth compensates for a messy compliance history.

> *In the world of institutional finance and serious investment, compliance is not a formality. It is the first filter. Before any investor, banker, or strategic partner looks at your business model, your growth, or your team—they look at whether you have been following the rules. If you have not, the conversation ends before it begins.*

The entrepreneur went back and spent six months cleaning up. By the time he was ready to approach investors again, the market window for his product had narrowed, a competitor had emerged, and the funding round he secured was at a lower valuation than he could have commanded eighteen months earlier.

Non-compliance does not just cost money. It costs opportunity. And missed opportunity, unlike a penalty, cannot be recovered.

The Smartest Investment You Will Ever Make

I want to reframe something that I hear constantly from business owners, especially early-stage ones.

"CA fees are expensive. Compliance is a cost I am trying to minimise."

Let me tell you what compliance actually is, in the language of a business owner who thinks in returns and investments.

Every rupee you spend on proper compliance today is buying you optionality for tomorrow.

- *It buys you the ability to walk into a bank and get a loan when you need to grow.*
- *It buys you the credibility to invite an investor into your business.*
- *It buys you the protection of never having a GST officer or income tax notice derail your operations at a critical moment.*
- *It buys you the ability to bid for government tenders, corporate contracts, and large institutional clients—all of whom will ask for clean compliance records before signing.*
- *And it buys you peace of mind—the ability to sleep without wondering if something you left unfiled is quietly becoming a problem.*

When I started my practice, compliance was seen as the boring end of the CA profession. The exciting work was in deals, mergers, fundraises, and advisory. And those things are exciting. But I have learned, over years of working with real businesses, that compliance is not the opposite of growth. It is the foundation of it.

Every large company you admire—every business that has taken institutional money, listed on a stock exchange, partnered with global brands—did it on the back of clean, consistent, unimpeachable compliance. Not because investors love paperwork. But because clean compliance is proof that the business is run by serious people who take their responsibilities seriously.

Compliance is not what you do after you grow. It is what you do to deserve to grow.

Five Things Every Business Owner Should Do Right Now

Let me close this chapter with practical guidance—not theory, not philosophy, but specific actions that will protect your business and give it the foundation it needs to grow.

- **File everything on time, every time:** Set calendar reminders for every GST return date, TDS deposit deadline, income tax due date, and ROC filing. These are non-negotiable. A reminder costs nothing. A late penalty costs real money.
- **Explore the Composition Scheme if eligible:** If you are a service business below fifty lakh turnover or a trader below one point five crore, check with your CA whether the Composition Scheme makes sense for you. The potential saving is significant.
- **Invest in tax planning, not just tax filing:** There is a difference. Filing is reactive—it records what happened. Planning is proactive—it shapes what will happen. Ask your CA specifically about legal tax planning strategies for your business structure. This conversation, done annually, can save you lakhs.
- **Choose your CA on quality, not price:** This is a decision that compounds. A CA who charges thirty thousand a year and does mediocre work will cost you far more in missed planning, late filings, and poor advice than a CA who charges one lakh and does exceptional work.

Your compliance partner is not a vendor. They are an investment.

- **Get your house in order before you need it:** Do not wait for the bank loan requirement or the investor's due diligence request to discover your compliance gaps. Do an annual compliance audit—every year, before March 31st—and close any open items proactively. When opportunity knocks, you want to be ready.

You did not read this book to run a small, compliant, mediocre business. You read it to build something real—something that grows, that lasts, that creates genuine wealth and freedom for you and your family.

Compliance is not the obstacle to that vision. It is the price of entry. Pay it willingly, plan it intelligently, and let it be the quiet, unshakeable foundation on which everything else you have learned in this book is built.

YOUR ACTION STEP–CHAPTER 9

This week, do a complete compliance health check on your business:

GST audit: Are all your GST returns filed and current? Log into the GST portal and check for any missing or pending returns. If there are gaps—call your CA today.

Income tax check: Are your income tax returns filed for the last three financial years? Is your advance tax being paid on time? If not, calculate the interest you are already accumulating.

TDS review: Is TDS being deducted correctly from payments to contractors, consultants, and rent? Is it being deposited by the 7th of every month? Errors here are costly and surprisingly common.

Composition Scheme eligibility: If you are a small business, ask your CA this week: am I eligible for the Composition Scheme, and would it benefit me?

Tax planning conversation: Book a one-hour tax planning session with your CA before the end of this financial year. Ask specifically: what can we do legally to reduce my tax liability this year? That one conversation is worth every rupee of the fee.

The business owner who treats compliance as an investment will always outlast the one who treats it as an inconvenience. Build on solid ground.

*

Coming up in Chapter 10:

The Power of Partnerships—How the right alliances can compress five years of growth into one

Chapter Ten

THE POWER OF PARTNERSHIPS

Everyone plans for what happens when things go wrong. Nobody plans for what happens when things go right—and that is where most partnerships break

Two Friends, One Business, and a Problem Nobody Prepared For

Two friends started a business together in 2018. Both were energetic, ambitious, and completely aligned—at least in the beginning. They complemented each other well. One was the relationship person, the other the operations person. Between them, they had everything a business needs to get started.

And get started they did. The early years were hard. Losses, thin margins, chasing every lead, learning as they went. But they stuck together through all of it. When things were bad, they were on the same side.

Then the business grew.

It crossed fifty crore in turnover. Then a hundred crore. By any measure, a remarkable achievement—two friends who had built something genuinely significant from nothing.

And that is precisely when things started falling apart.

Decisions that once took a five-minute conversation now carried the weight of crores. A one percent disagreement on margin policy was a one crore disagreement in rupees. Opinions on where to invest, which clients to prioritise, how much to draw from the business, when to hire senior leadership—every one of these conversations became a negotiation. And then an argument. And then a standoff.

When I sat with them, both deeply frustrated, I asked a simple question: what does your partnership agreement say about decision-making at this scale?

They looked at each other. Then back at me.

Their agreement—written with a lawyer's help back in 2018—covered what would happen if the business failed. What if one partner wanted to exit when the company was losing money. What if they had to wind down.

It said almost nothing about what would happen if they succeeded.

Everyone plans for failure. Nobody plans for success. And that is exactly where most partnerships break.

This is one of the most consistent patterns I see in business partnerships across India. The early agreements are built for the worst case—dissolution, loss, exit under stress. But no one sits and asks: what happens when we hit fifty crore? Who gets to make the call on a two-crore capital expenditure? What if one partner wants to expand aggressively and the other wants to consolidate? What if one wants to bring in an investor and the other does not?

These are not edge cases. These are the inevitable conversations that every growing business will have. And if you have not agreed on the answers in advance—calmly, clearly, in writing—you will have them under pressure. When crores are at stake. When egos are involved. When friendship has been stretched thin by years of shared stress.

That is not when you want to be figuring out the rules.

Story Two: The One Who Quit–and the Ones Who Did Not

Three friends decide to start a business. It is a great idea. All three are excited. But none of them wants to be the first to leave the security of their jobs.

So they make an arrangement. One of them—let us call him Rajan—quits his job to run the business full-time. The other two will continue working and support from the side—financially, with advice, with connections. And when the business is stable, they will all join.

Rajan agrees. He trusts his friends. They are all going to be equal partners. Thirty-three percent each. It is all agreed. Handshake. Done.

Rajan throws himself into the business. He takes a salary cut. He works sixteen-hour days. He handles the early client rejections, the operational chaos, the lonely months when nothing seems to be working. He builds the business from the ground up while his two partners continue drawing comfortable salaries from their jobs, occasionally joining calls and offering opinions.

Two years later, the business is doing well. Real revenue. Real clients. Real potential.

And now Rajan does not want to give thirty-three percent to each of his partners. Not because he is greedy. But because he has genuinely earned more. He was there every day. He took the risk. He built the thing. And they—whatever their original intentions—were not really there.

> This is one of the most common and painful partnership disputes I encounter. And it is almost always preventable. Not by choosing better friends. But by having better agreements—ones that account for contribution, not just ownership.

The original partners feel betrayed. "We had a deal," they say. "Equal partners." And they are right—that was the deal. But the deal was made before anyone knew what building the business would actually require. Before anyone knew that Rajan would be the one to carry it.

When I step into situations like this, there is no clean answer. The agreements were insufficient. The expectations were misaligned. And the friendship—which is often the most valuable thing at stake—is now in serious jeopardy.

Do not let this happen to you.

> *In his book 'The Hard Thing About Hard Things', Ben Horowitz writes about the brutal reality of co-founder disputes—that the relationship between co-founders is the most important and most fragile element of any early-stage business. He recommends radical clarity on roles, decision-*

making authority, and equity vesting before the business begins—not after it has proven itself.

The lesson is not that partnerships are bad. The lesson is that the structure of a partnership—how decisions are made, how contributions are valued, how equity is earned over time—must be discussed with the same seriousness as the business model itself. More, even. Because the business model can be pivoted. The ownership structure, once entrenched, is very hard to change.

Story Three: When Nobody Knew Who Was in Charge

A husband and wife started a business together. Both capable. Both passionate about the idea. Both had complementary skills that, on paper, made them an ideal founding team.

But they never clearly divided responsibilities. Marketing, operations, client relationships, finances—everything was shared, everything was discussed jointly, and most decisions required both of them to agree.

In the beginning, this felt like collaboration. Like true partnership.

A year in, it felt like everything needed two signatures—and one of them was never available when the other needed a quick decision. Clients waited for quotes that required both partners to review. Vendors were given conflicting instructions because both partners managed the relationship separately. The team had two bosses, both with authority, and no clear way to resolve when they disagreed.

The business was slowing down not because the market was bad, not because the product was weak—but because the internal decision-making was constantly gridlocked.

A business with two equal decision-makers and no agreed division of authority is not a partnership. It is a permanent negotiation.

The fix was not complicated. We sat together and mapped every function of the business—marketing, sales, operations, finance, HR, client management, strategy. And we assigned a primary owner to each one. Not the person who would do the work—but the person who had final authority to make decisions in that area.

Marketing and client relationships: her domain, final call.

Operations, finance, and compliance: his domain, final call.

Major strategic decisions above a certain threshold: joint decision, with a defined process for resolving disagreement.

Within a month, the business moved faster. The team had clarity. Clients got faster responses. And the partnership itself became healthier—because friction had been replaced with structure.

Clear boundaries do not weaken partnerships. They protect them.

Partnerships Beyond Co-Founders–The Collaboration Opportunity Most Businesses Miss

Everything we have discussed so far is about formal partnerships—co-founders, equity partners, joint ventures. But there is another category of partnership that most small and mid-sized businesses completely underutilise, and it is one of the fastest ways to grow.

Strategic collaborations.

Here is how I think about it.

You have identified your niche—from Chapter 2. You are good at two or three things and you serve a specific type of client. But your client, being a business owner themselves, has a dozen needs. They need legal advice, financial advisory, digital marketing, HR support, technical consulting, operational software, and more—in addition to whatever you specifically offer.

Right now, when a client asks you for something outside your niche, what do you do? Most service business owners either try to do it themselves—badly, expensively—or they say "I do not do that" and leave the client to figure it out alone.

Both are missed opportunities.

- *When you refer your client to a trusted collaborator who does excellent work in an adjacent area—you get goodwill, a stronger client relationship, and often a reciprocal referral.*
- *When your collaborators refer their clients to you for what you do—you get warm, qualified leads from someone whose recommendation carries weight.*
- *When you build a network of complementary professionals who serve the same niche—you collectively become a one-stop trusted resource for that niche. Clients stop looking elsewhere.*
- *And when you combine capabilities with a collaborator on a joint proposal—you can win mandates that neither of you could win alone.*

This is the kind of partnership that can compress five years of organic growth into one. Not because of luck, but because two credible, well-connected professionals working together reach twice the market with twice the trust.

I have built collaborations with legal firms, technology consultants, marketing agencies, and industry-specific advisors—all serving the same manufacturing and service business niche. Every referral I send builds a relationship. Every referral I receive is a warm, trust-backed lead. The network compounds.

Do not wait until you are large to start collaborating. Start now. Identify three to five professionals who serve your ideal client in a complementary way. Have a coffee. Understand their work. Send them a referral. Ask for nothing immediately. The relationship will produce returns in time.

What Every Partnership Agreement Must Address–Before You Start

Whether you are entering a formal co-founder partnership, a referral collaboration, or a joint venture—the conversation about terms must happen before the relationship begins. Not after it has grown complicated. Before.

And the most important conversations—the ones most people avoid because they feel awkward—are about what happens when things go right.

Here is a checklist of the questions every partnership agreement must answer:

- **Ownership and equity:** What percentage does each partner own, and on what basis? Is equity fixed or does it vest over time based on contribution?
- **Roles and authority:** Who is responsible for which function? Who has final decision-making authority in each domain? What decisions require joint approval?
- **Salary and drawings:** What does each partner draw as salary? How is this reviewed? What happens if the business cannot afford both salaries in a difficult month?
- **Profit distribution:** When and how is profit distributed? What percentage is reinvested and what is paid out? Who decides?
- **Dispute resolution:** If partners disagree on a major decision, what is the process? Is there a tiebreaker mechanism? An independent advisor who both trust?
- **New partner or investor onboarding:** What is the process if either partner wants to bring in a new investor or equity partner? Does the existing partner have right of first refusal?
- **Exit provisions—for success:** If one partner wants to sell their stake when the business is doing well, at what valuation? Who gets to buy first? How is the price determined?
- **Exit provisions—for failure:** If the business is wound down, how are assets, liabilities, and remaining cash divided?
- **Non-compete:** If a partner exits, can they start a competing business? For how long and in what geography?

- **Contribution milestones:** If a partner who was supposed to join full-time has not done so within a defined period, what happens to their equity?

These conversations feel uncomfortable before the partnership begins, because everything is hopeful and everyone is trusting. But that discomfort is precisely why you must have them then—when no one has anything personal at stake yet, and when every answer can be given with clarity and goodwill.

Once money is involved, once the business has grown, once personal lifestyles depend on the outcome—the same conversations become negotiations. And negotiations between partners who once trusted each other implicitly are among the most painful conflicts I have ever witnessed in business.

Have the hard conversation once, clearly, before you start. Or have it a hundred times, bitterly, after things go wrong.

Get the Structure Right–Partnership, LLP, or Private Limited

One more practical point before we close this chapter. The legal structure you choose for a partnership matters—not just for taxes and compliance, but for how disputes are resolved and how exit rights work.

General Partnership: The simplest structure, but the most dangerous. Partners have unlimited personal liability for the firm's debts. No separate legal identity. If the firm defaults, creditors can come after your personal assets. Avoid this structure for any business with significant revenue or risk.

Limited Liability Partnership (LLP): A more protected structure. Partners' liability is limited to their capital contribution. Separate legal identity. Easier to add or remove partners. Better suited for professional service businesses—consulting, legal, advisory.

Private Limited Company: The strongest structure for any business planning significant growth, external investment, or eventual sale. Shareholders' liability is limited. Equity can be structured with vesting clauses, investor rights, and preference shares. This is the structure that institutional investors and banks are most comfortable with.

Choosing the right structure at the right time is a conversation worth having with your advisor before you register. Changing structure later is possible—but expensive, time-consuming, and sometimes complicated by existing agreements.

Build the foundation right the first time.

Partnerships Are Powerful–When They Are Built With Clarity

I want to close this chapter by saying something clearly, because I do not want the cautionary stories to leave you with the wrong conclusion.

Partnerships are powerful. Some of the most successful businesses in India and the world were built by two or three people who brought complementary strengths, trusted each other enough to take a leap together, and created something that neither could have built alone.

The two friends who started their business in 2018 and built it to a hundred crore—that is an extraordinary achievement. The problems they faced were not because they were wrong to partner. They were because they did not prepare for success with the same thoroughness that they prepared for failure.

Rajan and his friends—their vision was right. Their process was incomplete. A clearer conversation before they started about contribution, vesting, and what happens when the business grows would have protected all three of them.

Every one of these stories has a version where it ends well. That version requires one thing: clarity. Clarity in roles, clarity in expectations, clarity in what success looks like and how the rewards of that success are shared.

Find your right collaborators. Build your referral network. Seek out partners who complement your strengths and share your values. Go into those relationships with open eyes, clear agreements, and the willingness to have the uncomfortable conversations early.

Done right, a great partnership does not just grow your business. It halves the burden, doubles the perspective, and makes the journey far less lonely.

And in business—as in life—the journey matters as much as the destination.

YOUR ACTION STEP–CHAPTER 10

This week, take stock of your partnerships—existing and potential:

If you have a business partner: Schedule a dedicated conversation—not about operations, but about the agreement. Go through the ten-question checklist in this chapter. For each question where you do not have a clear written answer, that is a gap that needs to be filled. Get a consultant involved if needed.

If you are planning to partner with someone: Before signing anything or making any commitments, have the full conversation about success conditions—not just failure conditions. What does the business look like at five crore? At twenty crore? Who decides what at each stage? Write it down and have it reviewed by an advisor.

For strategic collaborations: Identify three professionals who serve your ideal client in a complementary way. This week, reach out to one of them for a fifteen-minute coffee conversation. No agenda beyond understanding their work and exploring whether there is a natural fit for referrals.

Review your business structure: Have a conversation with your CA or legal advisor about whether your current business structure—sole proprietorship, partnership, LLP, private limited—is appropriate for where you are going. If you are planning to grow significantly or bring in investment, the structure needs to support that before it becomes necessary.

The best time to have the partnership conversation is before you need to. The second best time is today.

*

Coming up in Chapter 11:

The Milestone and Beyond—What changes when you hit your first crore in profit, and how to plan what comes next

Chapter Eleven

THE MILESTONE AND BEYOND

Everything you have built, everything you have learned, and everything that is waiting for you on the other side of one crore

Close Your Eyes for a Moment

I want you to stop reading for just ten seconds.

I want you to close your eyes and picture something very specific.

It is a Tuesday morning. Not a Monday, because Mondays still carry the weight of the week ahead. A Tuesday—settled, unhurried. You wake up without an alarm. You make your own tea or coffee, slowly, the way you like it. You sit somewhere quiet and you open your phone—not to check if anything has gone wrong, not to answer the first of twenty urgent messages—but to look at your business dashboard. And what you see makes you exhale.

Revenue is tracking to plan. Your team is at work. Your systems are running. Three new leads came in overnight—not because you chased them, but because your reputation and your content brought them to you while you slept. Your EA has cleared your calendar of everything routine. Your afternoon is free for one strategic conversation that could change the trajectory of the next two years.

You are not busy. You are purposeful.

You have a driver who picks up your children when you are in a meeting. You take proper holidays—not working holidays where you answer calls by the pool, but real holidays where your business does not need you for ten days and nothing falls apart. You invest a portion of your earnings every month into assets outside the business. Your family is proud of what you have built. And the people who work with you—your extended family—are growing alongside you.

This is not a fantasy. This is what a one-crore-profit business makes possible. Not eventually. Not someday. Within a realistic, achievable timeline—for someone who reads this book seriously and acts on what it says.

The first crore is not the destination. It is the door. And on the other side of that door is the life you started a business to live.

Why the First Crore Is the Hardest–and Why That Is Beautiful

I will not lie to you. The journey to your first crore in profit is difficult. Genuinely, meaningfully difficult. And I think it is important to say that clearly—not to discourage you, but because understanding why it is difficult will help you push through the moments when you want to stop.

The first crore is hard because you are building everything from scratch at the same time.

You are building your reputation while having almost none. You are generating leads while your network is still small. You are hiring your first team while you are still figuring out how to lead. You are building systems while you are still deep in operations. You are pricing with confidence while the fear of losing clients is still very real. You are posting content while people around you are still laughing. You are paying taxes and compliance costs while every rupee feels precious.

You are doing all of this simultaneously. Without a map. With imperfect information. And often, without anyone who truly understands what you are going through.

That is why so few people make it.

Not because they are not talented. Not because they are not hardworking. But because this journey requires something rarer than talent and harder than effort: the ability to keep going through the long middle—the phase where you have started but have not yet arrived, where you have invested but not yet reaped, where you are building in the dark, trusting that the light will come.

The first crore rewards the people who refuse to stop just before the breakthrough arrives.

But here is the beautiful part.

Every single thing that makes the first crore hard—the network building, the reputation work, the system building, the team training, the lead generation discipline, the pricing courage—all of it compounds. And once it has compounded to the point where you hit that milestone, it does not reset. It accelerates.

What Actually Changes When You Hit One Crore

Let me describe precisely what is different on the other side of this milestone—because this is what you are working towards, and it deserves to be seen clearly.

- **People know your name**—Your content, your reputation, your client results have been compounding. You no longer have to explain who you are in every room. People come to meetings already knowing your story.
- **Your network works for you**—The relationships you have been building—the collaborators, the referral partners, the happy clients—now actively send you business. Leads arrive without you chasing every one.
- **Your systems run the operations**—The SOPs you built, the team you trained, the processes you documented—they handle the day-to-day. You are no longer the most expensive coordinator in your business.
- **Your pricing is respected**—At one crore in profit, you have proven your value. The clients who work with you understand what they are getting. Price conversations are shorter and less painful.

- **The bank respects you**—Three years of clean returns, healthy profit, and consistent compliance make you a desirable borrower. Capital is now a tool you can use to grow—not a barrier you cannot cross.
- **You can hire your replacement**—You can now afford—and justify—hiring the person who does what you do, operationally. The person who handles client delivery, manages the team, and keeps the engine running while you work on the next horizon.
- **Growth becomes a choice, not a struggle**—You are no longer fighting to survive. You are deciding where to go next. The journey from one crore to ten crore is not ten times harder than zero to one crore. It is actually easier—because you are starting with everything the first crore built.

Jeff Bezos once said that the secret to success is not doing something no one else has done—it is doing something everyone knows they should do, relentlessly, for longer than anyone else is willing to. Your first crore is built on relentless fundamentals: a clear goal, a focused niche, consistent lead generation, courageous pricing, a strong team, smart systems, visible content, healthy profit, clean compliance, and trusted partnerships. None of these ideas is new. What is rare is the person who applies all of them, consistently, without quitting.

From One Crore to Ten–Why the Next Phase Is Different

Once you cross the first crore milestone, the game changes in a very specific way.

In the zero-to-one-crore phase, you are the business. Everything flows through you. Your relationships, your judgment, your hustle—these are the engine.

In the one-to-ten-crore phase, the business becomes the engine. And your job shifts from doing to designing. From executing to directing. From being indispensable to being irreplaceable—in a different way. Not because no one else can do the work, but because no one else can see the horizon the way you do.

- *You hire an Executive Assistant who manages your calendar, your follow-ups, your communications. You stop spending mental energy on scheduling and start spending it on strategy.*
- *You hire someone who can run your core operations in your absence—your operational second-in-command. You test them. You trust them. You let go.*
- *You collaborate with two or three high-quality partners who send you premium clients—and to whom you send the clients who are outside your niche.*
- *You invest in one or two marketing initiatives that build your brand beyond your immediate network—a podcast, a speaking engagement, a published book.*
- *You begin building wealth outside the business—systematically, every month—so that the business is not your only asset.*
- *You plan for ten crore with the same discipline and specificity that you planned for one crore, back when this journey began.*

The one-crore milestone is not the end of ambition. It is the beginning of a different kind of ambition. A more focused, more leveraged, more joyful ambition—because you are no longer fighting for survival. You are building for legacy.

The first crore proves you can do it. Every crore after that proves you know how to keep doing it.

The Ten Things This Book Has Asked of You

Before the final exercise, I want to bring the entire journey of this book into one place. Not as a summary—but as a promise. A commitment from you to yourself.

If you have read this far, you have been given a complete roadmap. Not theory. Not inspiration without action. A real, tested, ground-level map of how service and manufacturing business owners go from where they are to one crore in profit—and beyond.

1. **Set a real goal**—Not a vague wish. A specific, written profit target for this financial year—with a plan attached. Every decision your business makes should be filtered through this number.
2. **Find your niche and own it**—You cannot be everything to everyone. The deeper you go into your chosen niche, the faster your expertise compounds, your reputation spreads, and your pricing power grows.
3. **Work your leads deliberately**—Three meetings a week. A maintained lead sheet. Consistent follow-up. Specific referral asks. Your first crore is already inside your contact book—go find it.

4. **Charge what you are worth**—Underpricing is not humility. It is self-sabotage. Premium fees produce premium work, attract premium clients, and fund the team and systems you need to grow.
5. **Build a team worth building**—Your first hire frees you. Your second makes you scalable. Your third makes you replaceable—in the best possible way. The ceiling of your business is the ceiling of your team.
6. **Create systems before you need them**—Document the processes. Build the SOPs. Schedule your CEO Block. A business that runs without you is not a luxury—it is a design decision you make before you are forced to.
7. **Show up online, consistently**—Content is not marketing. It is reputation—built one post at a time, compounding over months and years into a flywheel that generates trust, referrals, and recognition.
8. **Track profit, not just revenue**—Turnover tells you how much passed through your hands. Profit tells you how much you kept. Know your margins, review them monthly, and let the numbers make decisions for you.
9. **Treat compliance as an investment**—Every rupee you spend on getting your legal and financial house in order is buying you optionality—for loans, for investors, for large clients, for peace of mind.
10. **Build partnerships with clarity**—Find your collaborators. Set clear terms. Plan for success as carefully as you plan for failure. No business that lasts was built entirely alone.

A Letter to the Person Who Started This Journey

I want to speak to you directly for a moment. Not as an author to a reader. But as someone who has sat across from hundreds of people exactly like you—people who had the drive, the talent, and the ambition, but not yet the roadmap.

I know how it feels to start a business and not know if it will work. I know the weight of the early months when the clients are few and the doubts are loud. I know the exhaustion of being in operations all day and then lying awake at night worrying about growth. I know what it is like to watch your peers seem to move faster, seem more certain, seem more successful—while you are still figuring out your pricing.

I have been there. Many of my clients have been there. And almost every one of them who stayed the course—who implemented even a few of the things in this book, consistently, for long enough—reached a point where the momentum shifted. Where business started feeling less like a struggle and more like a machine. Where they stopped being the person the business needed and became the person who decided where the business went next.

That shift is coming for you too. I am completely certain of it.

Not because you are lucky. Not because the market will cooperate. But because you are reading this book—which means you are the kind of person who invests in getting better. And in business, as in life, the person who keeps learning and keeps acting will always, eventually, outpace the person who stopped.

You did not pick up this book by accident. You picked it up because somewhere inside you, you already know you are capable of more. This book was written to tell you: you are right.

The first crore is waiting for you. Not as a gift. Not as luck. But as the result of everything this book has asked you to do—the goal-setting, the niche focus, the lead generation, the courageous pricing, the team building, the systems, the content, the compliance, the profit tracking, the partnerships.

Do the work. All of it. Consistently. Without quitting when it gets slow.

And one day—sooner than you think—you will wake up on a Tuesday morning, pour your tea, open your dashboard, exhale, and know: you are there.

And then the real adventure begins.

With belief in what you are capable of,

Your Author

Practicing CA | Business Growth Advisor | Author

THE FINAL EXERCISE

Your First Crore Blueprint—Write It Down, Make It Real

Every chapter in this book ended with an action step. This final exercise brings all of them together. Find a quiet hour. Put your phone away. Take this seriously—because what you write here is not homework. It is a declaration of intent to yourself.

Write your answers in full sentences. Not bullet points. Not single words. Full, committed sentences—the way you would speak if you were making a promise to someone you deeply respect.

1. **My Goal**

   Write your exact profit target for this financial year and the financial year after that.

   Then write: what will reaching this number make possible in my life that is not possible today?

   My profit target this year is:

   ___

The year after, I will grow it to:

____

Reaching this number will make possible:

____

2. **My Niche**

   Complete this sentence: I help ________ businesses solve ________ so that they can ________.

   Write the three words or phrases that you want people to associate with your name.

   I help:

   ____

   When people hear my name, I want them to think:

   ____

3. **My Lead System**

   Write the names of ten people you will reach out to this week for meetings or referrals.

Write the one specific referral question you will ask at every meeting.

Ten people I will contact this week:

The referral question I will ask every time:

---

4. **My Price**

   Write your current pricing for your main service.

   Write the price you will charge for your next proposal—the number that reflects your true value.

   Write one sentence you will say with confidence when a client asks why you charge more than others.

   My current price is:

   My new price will be:

When asked why, I will say:

---

5. **My First or Next Hire**

   Write the role that, if filled today, would free up the most of your time.

   Write what that person would do and what success looks like in that role.

   The role I will hire next:

   What this person will do:

   Success in this role looks like:

   ---

6. **My One SOP**

   Write the single most time-consuming task you will systemise this month.

   Write who will own it once the SOP is built.

The task I will document and delegate:

The person who will own it:

---

7. **My Content Commitment**

   Write the platform you will post on and how many times per week.

   Write the topic of your very first post—the one you will publish within 48 hours of finishing this book.

   I will post on ___ platform ___ times per week.

My first post will be about:

---

8. **My Profit Number**

   Write your net profit from last financial year.

   Write your target net margin for this year.

Write the date of your monthly profit review.

Last year's net profit:

My target net margin this year:

My monthly review date is the ___ of every month.

---

9. **My Compliance Commitment**

Write any compliance gaps you currently have and a deadline to close each one.

Write the name of the CA or advisor you will call this week.

Compliance gaps I will close:

I will call ___ by ___:

---

10. My Vision—The Tuesday Morning

Go back to the opening of this chapter. The Tuesday morning. The tea, the dashboard, the exhale.

Write your own version of that morning in as much detail as you can. Where are you? What do you see? What does your life look like at one crore in profit? Make it vivid. Make it personal. Make it feel real.

This is your north star. Read it every morning for the next ninety days.

On the day I hit one crore in profit, my life looks like this:

Now close the book. Go build.

The first crore is waiting.

www.ingramcontent.com/pod-product-compliance
Lightning Source LLC
LaVergne TN
LVHW100318210926
848480LV00003B/1169
* 9 7 9 8 9 0 4 7 9 9 9 8 4 *